Community Detection in Complex Networks

A Research View

Dr.G.T. Prabavathi

Dr.V. Thiagarasu

Published by

BONFRING®
Intellectual Integrity

Community Detection in Complex Networks-A Research View

Copyright © 2017 by Bonfring

All rights reserved. Authorized reprint of the edition published by Bonfring. No part of this book may be reproduced in any form without the written permission of the publisher.

Limits of Liability/Disclaimer of Warranty: The authors are solely responsible for the contents of the paper in this volume. The publishers or editors do not take any responsibility for the same in any manner. Errors, if any, are purely unintentional and readers are required to communicate such errors to the editors or publishers to avoid discrepancies in future. No warranty may be created or extended by sales or promotional materials. The advice and strategies contained herein may not be suitable for every situation. This work is sold with the understanding that the publisher is not engaged in rendering legal, accounting, or other professional services. If professional assistance is required, the services of a competent professional person should be sought. Further, reader should be aware that internet website listed in this work may have changed or disappeared between when this was written and when it is read.

Bonfring also publishes its books in a variety of electronic formats. Some content that appears in print may not be available in electronic books.

ISBN 978-93-86638-08-3

Authors

Dr.G.T. Prabavathi
Dr.V. Thiagarasu

Bonfring
309, 2nd Floor, 5th Street Extension, Gandhipuram,
Coimbatore-641 012.
Tamilnadu, India.
E-mail: info@bonfring.org
Website: www.bonfring.org
Phone: 0422 4213231

Preface

Networks are natural representation for various kinds of complex systems such as biology, computer science, sociology etc. Various networks like biological networks, computer networks, social networks and communication networks exhibit the property of community structure. Community detection has been widely used in social network analysis to study the behaviour and interaction patterns of people within the network. Overlap is an interesting characteristic that occurs in complex network structures.

This book covers the preliminary concepts of complex networks and communities. The book also explores the concepts and techniques in community detection and label propagation. This book presents an overall picture of the common disjoint community detection algorithms and an in-depth study of overlapping community detection algorithms. The motivation in writing this book is to provide a guideline for the researchers who are beginners in the field of community detection. It is hoped that this book caters the needs of researchers who are interested in identifying overlapping communities in social networks. There is a description of glossary of terms used in the book for quick reference.

Chapter I covers the basics of complex systems and the growth of the study of the complex systems. It provides a brief insight of the importance of the study of complex systems in the current decade. This chapter also highlights various features of complex systems and the importance of communities in complex systems.

Chapter II starts with the necessity of community detection in complex networks. The chapter also covers the essential features of communities and their desirable properties. The classification of community detection algorithms is also presented in the chapter.

Chapter III provides an introduction to the types of community detection algorithms. This Chapter provides a list of algorithms designed for detecting disjoint and overlapping communities. A detailed background study has been made on these two types of algorithms.

Chapter IV focus the major issues in testing the community detection algorithms. The chapter presents the need of synthetic and benchmark networks for testing. Common benchmarks are well explored. The community detection algorithms should be evaluated with a quality metric to show the goodness of the algorithm. Hence, the chapter also discusses the metrics used for evaluating disjoint and overlapping communities both for synthetic and benchmark graphs.

Chapter V introduces the basic concepts behind label propagation techniques for identifying communities in complex networks. The chapter reviews in detail about the methodologies used by various researchers for detecting disjoint and overlapping communities using label propagation algorithms. The efficiency of various label propagation algorithms is also presented.

Chapter VI discusses the necessity of multi-label propagation techniques for efficient identification of communities. The architecture of multi-label propagation is also presented. The variations that can achieve significant improvements in detecting communities is discussed.

Dr.G.T. Prabavathi
Dr.V. Thiagarasu

Acknowledgement

Many depts. of gratitude are incurred during the academic endeavour and it is difficult to list all of them. Some deserve special recognition without whose help this book many not has been completed. We express our deep sense of gratitude to the authorities of Gobi Arts & Science College for providing support and motivations in making this book a reality. Special thanks are due to all the faculty members of Department of Computer Science for the constructive suggestions.

Materials for many of the chapters in the book are based on the research papers published in the Journals. We thank the reviewers for the constructive comments and valuable guidance in improving the content of this book. Our special thanks to our family members for their affection throughout the writing of this book. We are also thankful to the publishers for bringing out the book in the commendable form. This book is dedicated to our loving family members.

<table>
<tr><td>Chapter</td><td align="center">Contents</td><td>Page No</td></tr>
</table>

I	**Complex Networks-An Insight**	**1**
	1.1. Complex Networks	1
	1.2. Properties of Complex Networks	4
	1.3. Communities	5
	1.4. Community Features	9
	1.5. Applications	12
	1.6. Social Networks	13
	1.7. Summary	15
II	**Community Detection in Complex Networks**	**16**
	2.1. Introduction	16
	2.2. Community Detection	17
	2.3. Types of Algorithms	19
	2.4. Summary	24
III	**Community Detection Algorithms**	**25**
	3.1. Disjoint Community Detection	25
	3.2. Overlapping Community Detection	30
	3.3. Summary	41
IV	**Benchmarks and Metrics**	**42**
	4.1. Benchmarks	42
	4.2. Metrics for Evaluation	45
	4.3. Summary	50
V	**Label Propagation Algorithms**	**51**
	5.1. Introduction	51
	5.2. Label Propagation	52
	5.3. LPA for Disjoint Community Detection	56
	5.4. Overlapping Community Detection	62
	5.5. Summary	69

VI   **Multi-Label Propagation**   70

    6.1. Multi-Label Propagation[MLPA]   70

    6.2. Basic Notations   71

    6.3. Multi-label Propagation Architecture   73

    6.4. Overall System Design   79

    6.5. Conclusion   79

Glossary of Terms

Index

References

CHAPTER I

COMPLEX NETWORKS-AN INSIGHT

The study of complex system investigates how relationships between parts of a system give rise to the collective behaviours of a system and how the system interacts and forms relationships with its environment. Complex systems are defined on the basis of different perspectives in different research contexts and they can be represented as complex network, such as the Internet, World Wide Web, Biological networks, Communication networks and Social networks. This Chapter presents an overview of complex networks and the importance of communities in complex networks. Properties and types of complex networks are also discussed in the chapter.

1.1.   Complex Networks

Complex networks is an active field of research within the interdisciplinary science of complex systems. Complex network is a structure made up of nodes, representing entities, and links or edges, representing relationships of interactions between entities (Boccaletti et al. 2006). A complex network is a mathematical model of interactional phenomena that takes place in the real world. The elementary parts of a complex network are called nodes and their mutual interactions are links.

In mathematics, the study of networks starts with graph theory which deals mostly with regular and abstract constructions which have little in common with real networks. A significant advancement in graph theory took place when Erdös and Rényi (1959) initiated the study of random graphs and proposed a random graph model (ER model) to generate random graphs. The term random graph refers to the disordered nature of the arrangement of links between different nodes.

ER model served as a model for real-world networks for several decades. In random graphs, the distribution of edges among the vertices is highly homogeneous i.e. the distribution of the number of neighbours of a vertex or degree is binomial. Hence, most vertices have equal or similar degrees. The ER models can be extended in a variety of ways to make random graphs, a better representation of real networks. The small world network model was introduced by Watts and Strogatz (1998) to describe the change from regular network to complete random network. It contains both the small-world property and a high clustering coefficient. The model is based on a rewiring procedure of the edges implemented with a probability.

A small-world network is a mathematical graph, in which most nodes are not neighbours of one another, but most nodes can be reached from the other node by a small number of steps. Small-world network is as a network where the distance between two randomly chosen nodes grows proportionally to the logarithm of the number of nodes in the network. The study of complex networks whose structure is irregular, complex and dynamically evolving in time, with the main focus moving from the analysis of small networks to that of systems with thousands or millions of nodes with a renewed attention to the properties of networks of dynamical units emerged after the study of small-world network model (Boccaletti et al. 2006).

Real-world networks were thought as random networks. This view changed when Barabási and Albert (1999) demonstrated that in real-world networks like internet and metabolic network, the distribution of number of links per node (degree) is different from what is expected in random networks. In a large random network, node degrees are distributed according to the normal distribution. But, in real-world networks such as man-made and biological networks, the degree distributions are in high level and heterogeneous in nature. The degree distribution is broad with a tail that often follows a *power law*. The large amount of work on the characterization of the topological properties of real networks has motivated the need to construct graphs with power law degree distributions. Graphs with a power law degree distribution can be simply obtained as a special case of the random graphs with a specific degree distribution.

Barabási and Albert (1999) pointed out the distribution of edges is globally and locally inhomogeneous which has high concentration of edges within the special groups of vertices and low concentration between these groups. According to Barabási et al. (2000), most real-world complex networks obeyed the power-law degree distribution instead of poisson distribution as in random networks. Since power-law distribution does not contain obvious feature length, such networks are always called *scale-free networks*. Barabási and collaborators coined the term *scale-free network* to describe the class of networks that exhibit a power-law degree distribution. Scale-free networks are networks in which growth of the network or aging processes do not play a dominant role in determining the structural properties of the network.

After the identification of scale-free networks which discusses about properties that do not occur in simple networks, i.e. random graphs, a lot of research has been progressed to identify such networks (Transportation networks, Internet, World Wide Web and Scientific citation networks) and to develop models for the networks. The study of scale-free networks triggered the study of complex networks in various domains after which network theory has developed rapidly for reviews by many authors (Albert and Barabási 2002; Newman 2003; Newman et al.

2006a). They proposed modifications and generalizations to make the model a more realistic representation of real networks. Physicists in particular, have become more interested in the study of networks that describe the topologies of a wide variety of systems such as the World Wide Web, social, communication networks, biochemical networks and many more.

To scientists across a variety of fields, the term network is interpreted with various perspectives. In addition to the developments in mathematical graph theory, the study of networks has seen important achievements in social sciences also. Sociologists recognized early that they needed powerful mathematical tools to address the challenging problem of formation of large-scale patterns. Scott (2000) identified that networks can be used as an efficient way to study empirical data which is a system of network of people and their relationships.

Sociologists modeled complex networks as a network of people and their relationships with statistical models (Carringtonet al.2005). Complex networks were used in the analysis of computer science too (Lynch1996), but limited to small data sets with strong focus on the properties of a single node. Due to the developments in computing and communication technology and the availability of efficient computational resources, the study of large scale complex networks was initiated in late 1990s. As the number and size of the network data increased, the interest in computational techniques to understand the properties and organization of networks also increased.

Many systems are actually organized as complex networks (Fortunato 2010; Donetti and Munoz 2004). Technological networks such as World Wide Web, Electric networks, Global transportation networks and Delay-tolerant networks (Radicchi et al. 2004); Biological networks such as Epidemic networks (Moore and Newman 2000; Pastor-Satorras and Vespignani 2001), Metablic networks (Ravasz et al. 2002) and Ecological networks (Garlaschelli et al. 2003); and Social networks, such as scientists' collaboration networks (Newman 2001), Online community networks and large organization networks are some examples of complex network.

The above said complex networks may contain millions of nodes with complex structures. Due to the complexity of node structures, both space and time complexity also increases in the learning process of these networks. Biological networks are distinct from social networks that are in turn quite distinct from information networks. Due to the heterogeneous nature of different networks, studying and analyzing the complex networks structure has become the key challenge for researchers. The methods of complex network research mainly focus on graph theory, statistical mechanics and social network analysis.

1.2.   Properties of Complex Networks

Path: A basic characteristic of a network is the average distance between all pairs of nodes or the maximum distance. A path in a network is simply a chain of links forming a connection between two nodes (Watts and Strogatz 1998). Length is the number of links on the path and the distance between two nodes is defined as the length of the shortest path connecting the nodes.

Degree distribution: The degree is the basic property measuring the number of neighbours of a single node i.e. the number of edges connected to a particular node. While characterizing the networks in the real-world, the simplest thing to measure is the degree of the vertex from which degree distribution can be easily calculated. The highest degree nodes are often called *hubs* as they have a central position in the network and have specific roles in their networks, which depend greatly on the nature of the network. Nodes more frequently connected to others are similar or different in some quality which is referred to as assortativity or disassortativity. In many biological networks, degrees are disassortative where high degree nodes systematically link to nodes of low degree. In social networks, degrees are highly assortative which means nodes with similar degree tend to link to each other.

Clustering coefficient: Clustering coefficient is a measure of the degree to which nodes in a graph tend to cluster together. Watts and Strogatz (1998) defined the clustering coefficient as "Suppose that a vertex v has k neighbours; then at most edges $k_v = k_v - 1$ can exist between them (which occurs when every neighbour of v is connected to every other neighbour of v). Let C_v denote the fraction of these allowable edges that actually exist. Then c is the average of C_v over all v ". Random graphs have a small clustering coefficient while real-world networks often have a coefficient which is significantly larger. In most real-world networks and especially in social networks, nodes tend to create tightly knit groups characterized by a relatively high density of ties.

Small-world effect: The tendency for individual elements in a large system to be separated from any other element in the system by only a few steps is called small-world effect. The small-world effect is found in many real-world phenomena like food chains, the connectivity of the internet, networks of brain neurons and social networks. In the context of a social network, small-world effect results in the small world phenomenon of strangers being linked by a mutual acquaintance. A graph is considered as small-world, if its average clustering coefficient is significantly higher than a random graph constructed on the same vertex set, and if the graph has approximately the same mean-shortest path length as its corresponding random graph.

Communities: Basic characteristic at the level of single node is degree and at the level of the entire network are correlation, clustering and path. A common topological feature among all kinds of networks is community structure. Networks, in nature, possess a remarkable amount of structure. The structure of most networks reveals a high order structures which reveals the functional organization of networks. In particular, vertices with similar properties have a higher chance to be linked to each other than random pairs of vertices thus forming highly cohesive subgraphs, which are called communities, clusters, cohesive groups or modules.

1.3. Communities

Among the various properties used to study complex networks, communities has become one of the most important property and identifying community structures in networks is an interesting step towards understanding the complex systems they represent. A community in a network can be viewed as *a group of nodes within which the network connections are dense, but between which they are sparse* (Girvan and Newman 2002). Figure 1.1 depicts a small network with three communities denoted by the dashed circles which have dense internal links but between which there are only a lower density of external links (Newman and Girvan 2004).

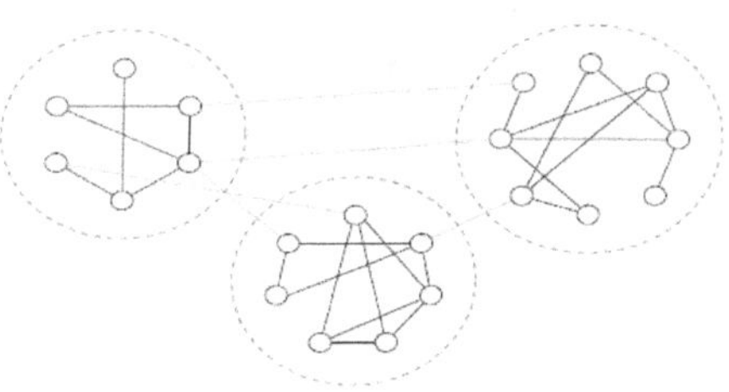

Figure 1.1: A Small Network with Three Communities (Newman and Girvan 2004)

Human are connected to relatives, friends and colleagues who are in turn connected to each other in groups of different sizes and cohesions. Considering an example of a network of the students of a college, where the nodes represent the students and links represent the connections if the corresponding students have met during a certain time period. Students belonging to same class or department or clubs are densely connected in the network, whereas connections between classes are sparse. In order to understand the relationships between the students in the network, all the vertices and edges of the network have to be analyzed which is impossible on large systems.

Communities help to have a compact and understandable description of a complex network as a whole. Hence, identification of communities hidden within the structure of complex networks is studied as a critical problem. Importance of communities in large networks has been studied by an interdisciplinary group of scholars, including physicists, mathematicians, biologists, engineers, social scientists and computer scientists.

Communities are closely related to functional units of the system. For example, groups of individuals interacting with each other in a society(Girvan and Newman 2002; Arenas et al. 2004; Palla et al. 2007b), the websites containing the related topics or similar themes may belong to the same community in World Wide Web (Gibson et al. 1998; Flake et al. 2002), functional modules such as cycles and biochemical pathways in metabolic networks (Guimera and Amaral 2005; Palla et al. 2005), proteins having the same specific functions within the cell group together as community in protein-protein interaction network (Chen et al. 2004) and dividing different nodes into different communities according to their inner propertiesin electric networks or biological networks (Milo et al. 2002). Nodes belonging to a tight-knit community in the above said complex networks are more likely to have common properties among them. Identifying the communities in the complex network, based on the common properties could simplify functional analysis of that network considerably.

There is no unique way to rigorously define what constitutes a community and no definition is universally accepted. Various definitions for community exist in the literature which depends on the specific system and application the researcher has in mind. Communities can be defined depending on whether:

- the network properties are viewed globally or locally?
- the nodes can simultaneously belong to several communities?
- the link weights are utilized or not?
- the definition allows for hierarchical community structure?
- iterative, splitting or merging approach is followed?

In spite of various definitions for community, the most widely accepted one is *"a set of nodes that are more strongly connected among each other than with the remaining part of the network"* (Newman and Girvan 2004).

Generally, communities are defined in two senses strong and weak communities. *Strong communities* are groups of nodes for which each node has more edges to nodes of the same community than to nodes outside the community (Flake et al. 2002). *Weak communities* are defined as a subgraph in which the sum of all node degrees within the community is larger than the sum of all node degrees towards the rest of the graph (Radicchii et al. 2004). Although, there are number of definitions for community, most of them state the notion that there must be more edges inside the community than edges linking vertices of the community with the rest of the graph (Fortunato 2010). This notion acts as a reference guideline for the most community identification problems.

Wasserman and Faust (1994) defined community as a *"subsets of actors among whom there are relatively strong, direct, intense, frequent or positive ties".*

Palla et al. (2005) defines the community in terms of cliques as *"A k-clique is a complete sub graph on k nodes (k = 3, 4,..,n), and two k-cliques are said to be adjacent, if they share exactly k-1 nodes".* The definition of clique is strict. When dealing with sparse networks which include only a few cliques, it is hard to find reasonable communities.

Gulbahce and Lehmann (2008) defined community as *"a densely connected subset of nodes that is only sparsely linked to the remaining network".*

Communities in graphs have been extensively investigated by (Fortunato 2010) and defined as *"a sub graph of a network whose nodes are more tightly connected with each other than with nodes outside the sub graph".*

Viewing the communities as clusters or modules, Fortunato (2010) further defines communities as *"groups of vertices that probably share common properties and/or play similar roles within the graph".*

Generally, community definitions can be done globally, locally or based on vertex similarity (Fortunato 2010). From the various definitions cited above, it can be understood that all definitions are quite similar but differ in their associated formal mathematical definition. The definitions are classified as:

Global

Global methods utilize the whole network structure for defining the communities. When clusters are essential parts of the graph, which cannot be taken apart without seriously affecting the functioning of the system, only global definitions suit for the community. Based on the assumption that a graph offers a community structure if it is not a random graph, then many global criteria are used to identify communities. In the global definitions, a global criterion is associated with the graph which is used to compute communities. This global criterion purely depends on the chosen algorithm.

A random graph that matches some structural properties of the original graph can be said as a *null model*. To find whether a graph exhibits community structure or not, null model is used as a term of comparison. Newman and Girvan (2004) proposed a most popular null model that consists of a randomized version of the original graph which formed the basics behind the definition of modularity. Modularity is a function which evaluates whether the partitions of a graph into clusters are good or not. It is one of the widely accepted global criterions to define a community and the key ingredient of the popular methods of graph clustering.

According to modularity, a subgraph is a community if the number of edges inside the subgraph exceeds the expected number of internal edges that the same subgraph would have in the null model. Many algorithms have been designed by using this global definition and several modifications and extensions of modularity definitions have been proposed in the literature of community detection.

Global methods have been popular in the past but there exists some problems in global definitions like resolution limits in modularity. Moreover, local methods are computationally more effective than global methods.

Local

The basic assumption of local methods is essentially local structures. Definitions based purely on local network structure have gained more popularity in the current decade. Local definitions study the inner structure of the remaining part of the graph independently. The study of local structures is preferable for large complex networks where each node does not depend on most of its peers. Particularly, a user in social network does not have any idea about how large the network is, but form topical communities based only on partial information.

Communities can also be defined by a fitness measure. The fitness measure expresses to which extent a subgraph satisfies a given property related to its cohesion. The larger the fitness, the community is more definite. Communities are defined based on quality functions also. Quality functions give an estimate of the goodness of a graph partition. Another important measure of interest for defining community is the relative density which is defined as the ratio between the internal and total degree of subgraph. A good community is expected to have a small number of edges joining it to the rest of the graph. Normally, communities should display more intra-group similarity than extra-group similarity. But, when a node belongs simultaneously to multiple communities, it displays more extra-group similarity than intra-group similarity (for example, ring communities stated by Goldberg et al. (2010)).

The methods that define communities through global objective functions like modularity may fail to discover the ring communities. Goldberg et al. (2010) viewed communities as a locally defined object and defined it as *"a set of members may qualify as a community independent of both the total communication intensity in the network and their memberships in other communities".*

Node Similarity

Communities can be assumed as a group of vertices similar to each other. The similarity between each pair of nodes can be computed with respect to reference property even if it is not connected by an edge. The similarity between nodes can be measured as the closeness between the pair of nodes. Using the node similarity, clusters are formed with a group of vertices that are most similar. Some of the popular similarity measures used in various community detection problems are distance calculations and random walks on graphs. If a network has a strong community structure, it takes a long time for a random walker inside a community to visit nodes randomly, due to the high density of internal edges in the community. The algorithms that follow random walks to detect communities, define community based on the measure which it follows.

1.4. Community Features

Various features are explored by various researchers in the field of community detection. Some of the important features such as hierarchy, overlapping, directed, weighted and dynamics are discussed below.

1.4.1. Hierarchy

When a node in a network belongs to only one community, then the community is said to be separated or disjoint. Most of the disjoint communities are hierarchical in nature. Hierarchy describes the organization of elements in a network. Hierarchies are common in human societies and are crucial for an efficient management of large organizations. This hierarchical partitioning process can then be represented by a tree or dendrogram as shown in Figure 1.2.

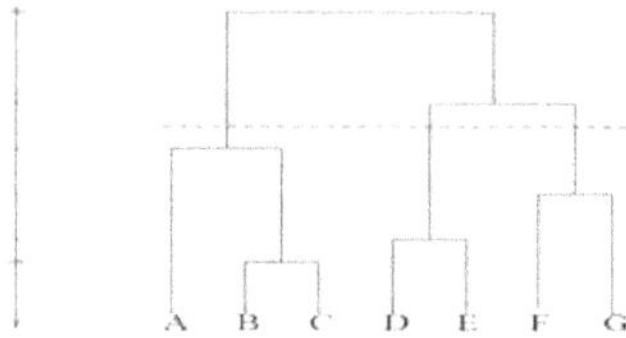

Figure 1.2: Hierarchical Representation of Communities as Dendrogram

(Newman and Girvan 2004)

1.4.2. Overlapping

The study on complex network models of real-world phenomena exhibit an overlapping community structure i.e. a node in the network can belong to more than one community. The presence of nodes belonging to several communities arises naturally from real data. Hence, overlap is one of the peculiar features of community. The overlap of different communities exists widely in real-world complex networks, particularly in social and biological networks. In complex networks, nodes are typically shared between two or more groups. In such cases, communities are said to be overlapping (the partitions becomes cover).Figure 1.3 shows the disjoint community structure and Figure 1.4 shows an example of possible overlapping of nodes by two communities.

Dense groups in complex networks often overlap with each other. For example, in social networks, human beings have multiple roles in the society and these roles make the members of network to join into multiple communities at the same time such as colleges, universities, families or relationships, companies, hobby clubs, etc., In biological networks, proteins involve in multiple functional categories. In co-authorship network, nodes represent the scientists and two nodes are connected if they have coauthored one or more articles and the articles are communities. Overlapping considerably increases the complexity of the communities.

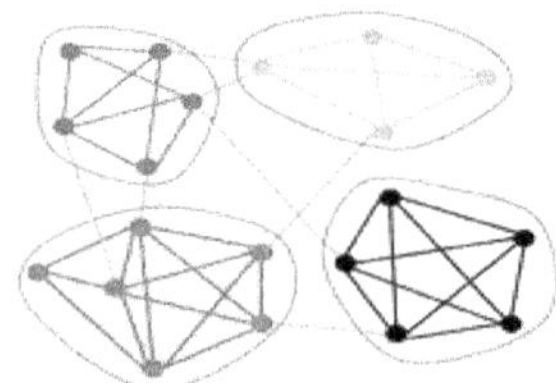

Figure 1.3: Disjoint Communities (Nguyen et al. 2011)

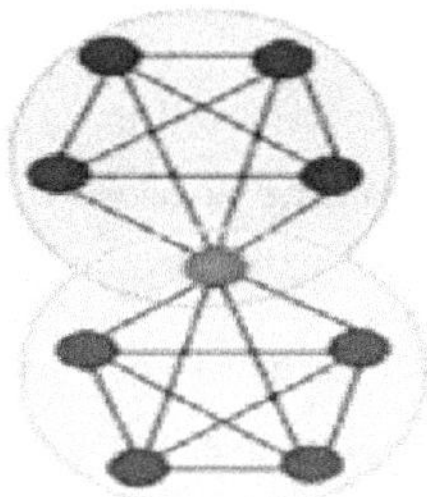

Figure 1.4: Overlapping Communities (Lazar et al. 2010)

1.4.3. Directed

Some real-world networks are represented with edges and links that are not reciprocal. For example, in the case of web pages, a hyperlink from one page to another is directed and other page may or may not have a hyperlink pointing in the backward direction. In the study of communities, direction of edges also plays an important role.

1.4.4. Weighted

A weighted network is a network where the links among nodes have weights assigned to them. In many real-world networks, not all links in a network have the same capacity. Links in complex networks are often associated with weights that differentiate them in terms of their strength, intensity or capacity. In social networks, the strength of social relationships is a function of their duration, emotional intensity, intimacy and exchange of services (Granovetter 1973). For non-social networks, weights often refer to the function performed by links such as between species in food webs or the amount of traffic flowing along connections in transportation networks. In weighted networks, a group of vertices can be considered as a community only if the weights of their connections are strong enough.

1.4.5. Dynamic

Complex networks are not always static. In reality, networks gradually evolve over time. Particularly, social networks witness the expansion in size and space as their users continuously increase and decrease, changing the network to dynamic in nature. A dynamic network is a special type of evolving complex network where changes are often introduced over time. The set of edges appearing and disappearing in the communities as time evolves have a little effect to the local structure of the network. But, over a long period of time this dynamics may lead to a significant transformation of network community structure. The study of dynamic communities is an emerging area of interest in the field of complex networks.

1.5. Applications

Finding the communities in the network have many applications including improving search engines, graph visualizations, realizing the network structure and detecting groups of special interest. Few applications are:

- Communities help to identify functional subunits of the system and to identify similarities among nodes that are not apparent in the absence of non-topological information. It uncovers relationships between the nodes which are not revealed by inspecting the network as a whole. In World Wide Web, identifying web client communities which have similar interests help the web service providers (phone, banking etc) to improve the services provided to the customers (users). For example, grouping the customers in web with interests on a specific product (prediction from the user searches in web) helps the online retailers for effective online marketing such as placing online advertisements and to recommend the list of items to the customers who are interested in that product and thus business opportunities are enhanced.

- Nodes from a community can be classified in accordance with their position (leaders, linking edges and so on). Identifying communities and their boundaries helps the classification of nodes, according to their structural position in the modules in social and metabolic networks. The nodes which share a large number of connections with the other group of partners occupy the central position in the community (core). Nodes in the core of the cluster may have a function of control on the stability of the group. Nodes lying at the boundaries between communities play the role of mediators between two different communities. In social networks, identifying such core and boundary nodes help to propagate messages.

- The community structure of a network can also act as a powerful visual representation of the system. In large networks, it is impossible to visualize all the vertices and edges of the network. Instead of visualizing the whole network, communities and their mutual connections can be displayed to have a more compact and understandable description of the network as a whole.

- In biochemical or neural networks, communities may be functional groups and separating such groups could simplify the functional analysis of the network.

- The identification of graph communities is applied in parallel computing too. For example, to decide what is the best way to allocate tasks to processors so as to minimize the communications between processers and perform calculations quickly. Nodes in these types of networks are computer processors that can be grouped into communities such as the number of physical connections between processors of different groups is minimal.

- Community structure proves to be extremely helpful in forwarding and routing strategies in communication networks.
- To understand dynamic processes taking place on the network like spreading of diseases that considerably affect the modular structure of the network.

1.6. Social Networks

The term social networking was first coined by Barnes in 1954. In World Wide Web, a social community is formed by people those who are having common ideas about a subject, sharing hobbies, working together etc. When the communities formed by the nodes of a network are modeled as a structure, it is represented as a complex network called as social network. The advancement of the information age has opened new possibilities in the field of social network analysis. Due to the availability of very large repositories of data stored in centralized location, researchers are provided with rich and publicly observable data to use in the analysis of social interactions.

Social Network Analysis (SNA) is an emerging area of interest due to the tremendous social networking services emerged as an important forum for expressing the thoughts of individuals in web. Social networking systems started with physical systems (Transportation and Energy networks), then continues through virtual systems (Internet, WWW, telecommunication), social networks, biological networks, etc. A social network is a social structure made of nodes (individuals or organizations) that are related to each other by various interdependencies like friendship, kinship, etc. Social networks have variety of different definitions (Wasserman and Faust 1994; Scott 2000) and might have different meanings depending on the nature of network such as scientist collaboration networks (Newman 2001) and friendship network of students (Amaral et al. 2000). Social networks include disease transmission networks, corporate networks, the spread of computer viruses, terrorist networks, online community networks and so on.

The elementary units of the social network can be defined as simple points called vertices (nodes), while their pair-wise relationships or interactions are said as edges (or links). Social network is considered as a collection of nodes which has data objects formed from social media or social individuals, connected by a set of edges, which represents the relationships between individuals. The relationships can be pair-wise interactions, liking or co-occurrences

(Jian et. al. 2009). Each edge represents the social relationships between two nodes representing people or objects.

In the study of social networks, the first question that arises is how to extract meaningful knowledge from the abundant data. As social network data grew far beyond the possibility of manual processing, the need for developing computationally efficient and accurate algorithms have raised. An algorithm that identifies the higher-order structures that is hidden within the networks gives meaningful insights about the functional organizations of the network. From the functional organizations interpreted, many actions can be taken such as marketing plans; advertising strategies; recommendations to users, etc. The higher order structures of network called communities reduce the complexity of a network and provide semantic knowledge about the network.

A social community is formed in web by people having common ideas about a subject, sharing hobbies and working together. If the above said social communities are modeled as a structure in complex network, it forms social network. In social network, people like to find new friends, write new comments on their friends' view or read the comments of friends about their view. Depending upon these activities, relationships among the social network users are established. As the activities grow, the relationships between like-minded users grow. Depending upon the relationships, automatically communities are formed in social network.

Social networks are paradigmatic examples of graphs with communities. Communities in social networks can provide insights about common characteristics or beliefs among people which makes them different from other communities. The word community itself refers to a social context (Fortunato 2010). Communities in social networks depend on the observed interactions between people. People naturally tend to form groups with family, friends, within work environment etc. Social networks simulate this tendency and play an increasingly important role in web.

In social networks, individuals easily share their opinions and experiences globally. The necessity to extract communities based on these shared information is becoming vital for wide variety of applications. Algorithms for community detection within social networks have garnered significant interest in the past decade (Donetti and Munoz 2004; Baumes et al. 2005a; Clauset 2005; Gregory 2007; Lancichinetti et al. 2008).

Detection of communities within social networks is a non-trivial problem. Allowing communities to overlap further complicates the problem. In social networks, a social community usually consists of people sharing common interests who tend to interact more frequently with other members in the same group than to the outside world. Hence, it is natural that people do belong to multiple social groups simultaneously and being able to detect overlapping communities is an important step to understand and analyze social networks.

In online social networks, mostly users participate in various social activities like connecting with other like-minded people, updating the status of photos, tags and so on. The diversity of people's interest and social interactions suggest that the community structures overlap. A user socially interacts with multiple groups based on the necessity, personal preferences and interests. So, individuals in this type of network naturally belong to more than one community such as community of family members, community of friends, community of colleagues and also communities based on several interest-based affiliations. The concept of "circles" in Google and "smart list" in Facebook explicitly implement this idea.

Due to the tremendous growth of internet, popularity of social networking websites and the parallel development of communication technologies like smart phones, there is a high demand for identifying communities and their overlapping structure. Since, the extracted community information can be commercially used for advertising; community detection in social network has emerged as an interesting area of research.

1.7. Summary

Many complex systems can be described as networks and the analysis of networks using tools borrowed from graph theory has proved to be a useful approach in studying the complex systems. The problem of dividing a graph into interesting subgraphs is a classical problem in graph theory and various reasons and motivations are there for cutting a graph into smaller components. Communities naturally arise as a consequence of simple interactions among people and do not require complicated mechanisms to be obtained and have many useful properties such as high internal connectivity and high robustness which are essential for real applications. Communities in social networks depend on the observed interactions between people. The necessity to extract communities based on these shared information is becoming vital for wide variety of applications. This chapter presents an introduction to complex networks, properties of complex systems, the importance of communities and the growth of social network communities.

CHAPTER II

COMMUNITY DETECTION IN COMPLEX NETWORKS

This chapter covers the necessity of community detection in complex networks. The categories of community detection and the essential properties of the community detection algorithms are discussed. Four categories of algorithms that are commonly used in the field of community detection are listed.

2.1. Introduction

As complex networks are made up of large number of nodes, detecting and analyzing the community structures may lead to an improved understanding of the overall network system. The basic assumption of any community detection algorithm is that the underlying nodes in the network structure may tend to form communities and it should be identified. Therefore, community detection in complex networks is an important and interesting problem. The problem of community detection in complex networks arises in various domains and is studied in many diverse research fields such as physics, sociology and computer science where networks are often represented as graphs.

Detecting the correct communities are of critical importance and an algorithm that detects communities in complex networks should aim to accurately group the communities as expected. The number of applications of community detection in complex networks, especially in the knowledge extraction task in social and information networks has triggered the researchers to devise new community detection algorithms. The research for efficient community detection algorithms have attracted much interest in this decade than last decade due to the increasing availability of large network datasets and the increasing impact of networks on day to day life.

The research on community detection in complex network is classified into two categories.

- Disjoint communities which deal with nodes that belong to only one community.
- Overlapping communities in the network where nodes belong to more than one community.

When networks have structures, where a clear assignment of a node to a community is not possible or not desirable, then, the necessity of overlapping community detection algorithms arises. Usually, in social networks people are part of several natural groups. When a community detection algorithm assigns a node to exactly one community, the multitude of social embedding's cannot be represented properly. The nodes that are shared by several communities play a key role as intermediate between communities and the nodes predict dynamic behaviours of individual nodes in the network. The intermediate nodes are interesting to investigate. When a disjoint community detection algorithm is applied to a network which contains overlapping communities, it shall misleadingly classify overlapped nodes into different communities and fail to reveal the original network's structure.

Taking into account, the dynamics of network, the research on community detection can be further categorized as static and dynamic.

- If networks are static, the community detection algorithms aim to find static communities from the given static network.

- In dynamic networks, the community structure changes from time to time. In such case, static community detection algorithms cannot find meaningful communities from dynamic networks and so, the necessity of dynamic community detection arises. Hence, numerous community detection algorithms have been developed dealing with disjoint, overlapping, static and dynamic networks.

2.2. Community Detection

The problem of network representation is very complex and contains different variants in the traditional graph model. Each algorithm in the literature focuses on few properties of complex networks and establishes, explicitly or implicitly, its own definition for community and extracts communities, which typically reflect only part of the features of real communities on which it is based upon. The investigation of network community structure which is a more general form of data clustering has captured the attention of diverse group of scientists (Fortunato and Castellano 2009; Gulbahce and Lehman 2008; Schaeffer 2007). Due to the breadth of interest drawn from researchers in statistical physics, discrete mathematics, computer science, sociology and other subjects various algorithms have been proposed in the last decade.

Community detection is an interdisciplinary endeavor that makes the problem of detecting communities so challenging and requires domain-specific knowledge. Though communities have a long history in social science, the seminal paper of Girvan and Newman (2002) triggered a lot of interest on the problem of community detection. After the study of community identification by Girvan and Newman (2002), extensive studies were made in the area of community detection, mainly in physics and computer science.

Traditional Clustering Vs Community Detection

The focus of community detection has shifted away from the traditional clustering problem to finding group of nodes based on interactions and relationships between nodes in a network.

- The main aim of clustering is to find group of objects with common attributes.
- The objective of community detection is to find the interactions and relationships between the objects. This shift has caused the network to be viewed as a graph.

Desirable Properties of Community Detection Approach

Community detection algorithms can be classified into different techniques depending upon various features. These features can specify constraints for input data and can improve the power of the results. Though, there are various properties desirable for community detection approach, Coscia et al. (2011) listed the following as important features:

a. Parameter Free

In data mining research, an interesting feature of an algorithm is the absence of parameters. An algorithm should be able to make explicit knowledge that is hidden inside the data without getting any external information from the user regarding the data or the problem. For example, in community detection research, many algorithms expect the number of communities to be found as a parameter before executing the algorithm. But, there are certain algorithms that detect communities in the network without expecting the number of communities. An efficient community detection algorithm should attempt to detect communities without getting any external parameter from the user or try to minimize the number of parameters.

b. Multi-dimensional Input

If a complex network contains different kinds of relations established between the nodes of the network then it is said to be multi-dimensional. When dealing with multi-dimensions, the notion of community changes and the algorithms that are designed for simple static networks cannot handle the multiple dimensions of the network relations.

c. Incremental

An incremental algorithm should be able to provide an output without an exhaustive search of the entire input. As time evolves, the network structure may change by addition of nodes or removal of nodes. Incremental algorithms modify the community structure by looking only at its neighbourhood. A new node entering in the network should be placed in one of the previously defined communities without starting the community detection process from the beginning. This type of technique is suitable only for dynamic networks.

d. *Multipartite*

In general, networks consisting of different types of nodes with edges running onlybetween unlike types are called multipartite networks, of which the bipartite graph is a special case. The tremendous growth of real-world networks has forced the research community to develop scalable approaches that can be applied to complex networks with several millions of nodes and billions of edges. Many algorithms have been proposed to deal with community structure detection based on the principles such as hierarchical clustering, graph clustering, optimization methods, spectral partitioning of the network and many more. Depending on the criteria selection, one algorithm can belong to more than one category (Lancichinetti and Fortunato 2009b).

2.3. Types of Algorithms

Given the various choices in defining a community, it is natural that a large number of methods and related algorithms have been proposed over the years using a variety of techniques. Each algorithm has a view about the relation that exists between communities in the network. Depending upon the view of the researcher about the relation between communities, community detections algorithms can be classified into variety of techniques. Before discussing about various algorithms, it is necessary to have an overview of the types of algorithm. This section discusses few classifications of community detection algorithms.

An excellent review exploring the most popular types of community detection techniques was presented by Fortunato (2002). In the last decade, several reviews of community detection types have been published (Danon et al. 2005; Schaeffer 2007; Fortunato and Castellano 2009; Porter et al. 2009; Coscia et al. 2011). Coscia et al. (2011) characterized community identification basedon Feature Distance, Internal Density, Bridge Detection, Diffusion, Closeness, Structure Definition, Link Clustering and Meta Clustering.

The vast majority of algorithms (Girvan and Newman 2002; Newman and Girvan 2004; Clauset et al. 2004) assume that nodes in a network are members of a flat set of disjoint communities. This assumption is reasonable for many networks. For example, many employees work for a single employer, many papers published in a single conference and so on. Some algorithms (Palla et al. 2005) allow communities to overlap, with each node possibly appearing in more than one community. This type of relation is more realistic in certain cases like a researcher belongs to more than one research community; a person belongs to multiple hobby groups, etc.

Few algorithms aim to detect a *hierarchy* of communities. For example, research communities can be divided into several research groups. Thus, based on these views, numerous community detection algorithms have been developed using a variety of techniques: removal of *edge-betweenness* (Girvan and Newman 2002); *modularity optimization* (Newman 2004; Guimerà et al. 2004); *detection* of *dense subgraphs* (Palla et al. 2005); and *statistical inference* (Hofman and Wiggins 2008). This section describes four important categories of community detection algorithms.

a. *Graph Partitioning*

Graph partitioning is suitable for understanding the entire structure of networks, especially for the networks with a small size. In mathematics, the graph partition problem is defined on data represented in the form of a graph $G(E,V)$ with V vertices and E edges, such that it is possible to partition G into smaller components with specific properties. For instance, a k-way partition divides the vertex set into k smaller components. The network partitioning problem is generally defined as the partitioning of a network into c (a fixed constant) groups of approximately equal sizes, minimizing the number of edges between groups. A partition is said to be good, if the number of edges running between separated components is small. Network partitioning problem is considered as NP-hard and efficient heuristic methods have been developed over years to solve the problem (Kernighan and Lin 1970). Important applications of graph partitioning include scientific computing, task scheduling in multi-processor systems, clustering and detection of cliques in social and biological networks.

Partitional clustering finds clusters in a set of data points that are embedded in a metric space, so that each node is a point and a distance measure is defined between pairs of points in the space. The distance is a measure of similarity (or dissimilarity) between nodes. The number of clusters is pre-assigned and the goal of the partitional clustering is to separate the points in the pre assigned clusters such that the cost function is minimized or maximized. Commonly used functions are k-clustering, k-center and k-median. The limitation of partitional clustering is same as that of the graph partitioning technique i.e. the number of clusters must be specified at the beginning itself. Graph partitioning and community detection share the same objective of partitioning network nodes into groups. The number of clusters are predefined or given as input in graph partitioning techniques. But, in community detection, the number of communities in a network and their sizes are not known beforehand, but should be automatically searched (Flake et al. 2002; Radichii et al. 2004).

b. *Hierarchical*

The detection of the community structure in a network is generally intended as a procedure for mapping the network into a tree where the leaves are the nodes and the branches join nodes or (at higher level) groups of nodes, thus, identifying a hierarchical structure of communities nested within each other. Hierarchical clustering is a popular community detection technique that derives its name from its function of building a hierarchy of clusters. Much of the research in community detection treats the problem of locating communities as a hierarchical partitioning problem.

The hierarchical community detection algorithms assume the community structure of a network to be hierarchical i.e. individuals' form disjoint groups which become sub groups of larger groups until a single group is formed. This type of assumption is valid for some type of networks like organizational networks. For example, students in the same classes often form some strong local communities while these communities, for instance of same school, in turn form a larger but relatively weaker community. Hierarchical clustering is mainly applied to analyze the similarity of connections between each node in the network.

In hierarchical clustering, first a similarity measure is chosen and the similarity between each pair of vertices is calculated and a new similarity matrix is formed at the end. Hierarchical clustering is a popular community detection method such in social network analysis, biology and marketing because in addition to providing the identification of communities in the network, it also provides a hierarchical structure in the communities.

Hierarchical clustering does not require a preliminary knowledge on the number and size of the clusters, but the vertices of a community may not be correctly classified and the result purely depends on the similarity measure chosen. Hierarchical clustering technique is classified into Agglomerative clustering where clusters are iteratively merged and Divisive Algorithms where clusters are iteratively split by removing edges connecting vertices with low similarity (Fortunato 2010).

c. *Agglomerative*

Agglomerative clustering begins with every node in its own cluster and then iteratively merges clusters together by adding edges back into the network, based on a quality measure. The nodes are grouped into larger and larger communities and this procedure can be halted at any point and the resulting components in the network are taken to be the communities. Alternatively, the entire progression of the algorithm from empty graph to complete graph can be represented in the form of a tree or dendrogram. Horizontal cuts through the tree represent the communities appropriate to different halting points. Agglomerative methods based on a wide variety of similarity measures have been applied to different networks. Complex networks have natural similarity metrics built in. For networks which have no natural metric, it can be devised using correlation coefficients, path lengths or matrix methods.

d. *Divisive*

Detecting the edges that connect vertices of different communities and removing them is the technique followed by divisive algorithms. In divisive algorithms, the order of construction of the tree is reversed i.e. starting with the whole network, iteratively edges are removed (cut) dividing the network progressively into smaller and smaller disconnected networks. These smaller networks are identified as the communities. The most popular divisive algorithm by Girvan and Newman (Girvan and Newman 2002) triggered the interest of various researchers in the field of community detection. The authors used a measure called edge centrality to estimate the importance of edges. The output of the divisive algorithm can be easily represented through dendrogram which is easy for visualization also. The crucial point in a divisive algorithm is the selection of the edges to be removed which have to be those connecting communities and not those within them.

e. *Modularity Optimization*

A metric is necessary to measure how well the communities are detected or how it is progressing. In the absence of such metric, most algorithms would either continue until every node in the network is split into a single community or all nodes in the network join together into a single community. A stopping criterion proposed by Newman and Girvan (2006c) is called modularity (Q). The definition of modularity states that a network is *modular* when the actual number of connections among nodes in a partition is higher than the expected for a corresponding random graph, when the random graph is selected as the reference null model. If an algorithm takes modularity as the relevant metric, the community detection algorithm is said as modularity optimizing algorithm.

Modularity is used widely used as an objective function to optimize and also as a measure to compare the quality of the partitions obtained by different algorithms. The modularity value of a partition does not have a meaning by itself. Modularity acts as a quality function, only if it is compared with the corresponding modularity expected for a random graph of same size

(Reichardt and Borhnoldt 2006). High values of modularity indicate good partitions. Hence, the partition corresponding to a maximum probability values on a network should be best or at least a very good one (Fortunato 2010).

Obtaining high value of modularity has been the main objective of all modularity maximizing algorithms. Modularity optimization is a NP-complete problem (Brandes et al. 2008). Hence, it is not possible to find the exhaustive optimization value. But, there are number of algorithms that find fairly good approximation of the maximum modularity with least computational costs. The algorithms that approach modularity maximization for community detection fall under variety of techniques. Three common techniques that are commonly used are discussed below.

- *Greedy Optimization*: First Newman (2004) devised an algorithm to maximize modularity using greedy method. Clauset (Clauset et al. 2004) suggested that the updating operations performed by Newman (2004) can be performed using max-heaps to improve the run-time of the algorithm. Danon et al. (2006) normalized the modularity variations by merging the two communities using the fraction of edges incident to one of the two communities. Blondel (Blondel et al. 2008) introduced a different greedy approach for weighted graphs using sequential sweeps over all vertices.
- *Simulated Annealing*: It is a probabilistic procedure for global optimization. It consists of performing an exploration of the space of possible states, looking for the global optimum of a function at its maximum. Guimera et al. (2004) performed local moves where a single vertex is shifted between clusters at random and global moves consisting of merging and splitting of communities. Simulated annealing is slow and can be useful for small graphs only.
- *External optimization*: It is a heuristic search procedure by Boettcher and Percres (2001) to get good modularity with improved computer time. Duch and Arenes (2005) found the local modularity of a vertex based on the optimization of local variables, expressing the contribution of each unit of the system to the global function at study.

f. *Spectral Clustering*

A technique that partitions a set into clusters by using eigenvectors of matrices is called spectral clustering. It consists of a transformation of the initial set of objects into a set of points in space that coordinates elements of eigenvectors. The set of points is then clustered using standard techniques like k-means clustering. Spectral clustering is able to separate data points that could not be resolved by applying directly k-means clustering.

2.4. Summary

This chapter introduced the necessity of community detection in the field of complex networks. The desirable properties of community detection were highlighted and an overview of broad classification of community detection is given. Although there are various types of community detection approaches, in this chapter the four commonly used approaches for identifying communities are given.

CHAPTER III

COMMUNITY DETECTION ALGORITHMS

Depending on the structure of the network, community detection algorithms can be classified as disjoint and overlapping. Numerous algorithms have been proposed for detecting both disjoint and overlapping communities on static networks and dynamic network. A detailed list of most popular disjoint and overlapping community detection algorithms designed for static networks are listed in this chapter.

3.1. Disjoint Community Detection

This section reviews some disjoint community detection algorithms that are frequently referred in the literature of the community detection.

The most popular divisive algorithm GN proposed by Girvan and Newman (2002) marked the beginning of a new era in the area of community detection. After the publication of this algorithm, community detection turned as a topic of interest among physicists and applied mathematicians all over the world and numerous methods were developed addressing this problem. The main focus of GN algorithm is edge betweenness, which represents the number of shortest paths between pairs of vertices that run along an edge. If there exists more than one shortest path between a pair of vertices, each path is given equal weight such that the total weight of all of the paths is unity. If a network contains communities that are connected by a few intergroup edges, all shortest paths between different communities must go along one of these few edges. So, the edges connecting communities will have high edge betweenness. By removing these edges, groups are separated from one another to reveal the underlying community structure of the graph. GN finds the edges with highest edge betweenness and removes them to construct communities.

First step of GN calculates betweenness scores for all edges in the network. Second, the edge with the highest score is removed from the network. For all the remaining edges in the network, betweenness is recalculated followed by the removal of edges with highest betweenness score. The process is repeated until no edges remain in the network. The GN algorithm was the first to recognize that the centrality score must be recalculated after each edge removal. The output of the algorithm is in the form of a dendrogram which represents an entire nested hierarchy of possible community divisions for the network. The two principle disadvantages of this algorithm are:

(i) due to recalculation of centrality, it has high time complexity which limits this algorithm to small scale of networks

(ii) it provides no guide to how many communities a network should be split into.

Tyler et al. modified the GN algorithm, to improve the speed of the calculation (Tyler et al. 2003; Wilkinson and Huberman 2004) by applying Monte Carlo method to calculate edge betweenness. In the modified algorithm, edge betweenness was calculated only from a limited number of centers, chosen at random, deriving a sort of Monte Carlo estimate and used a stop criterion to end the process. The Monte Carlo sampling of the edge betweenness necessarily induces statistical errors. As a consequence, the partitions are in general different for different choices of the set of center vertices.

Communities are formed by a high density of edges and it is natural to expect that such edges form cycles and the edges lying between communities will hardly form cycles. Based on this concept, Radicchi (Radicchi et al. 2004) proposed an algorithm that is similar to that of Girvan and Newman (2002), based on iterative removal of edges. But, the algorithm uses a different measure instead of betweenness centrality to identify the edges to be removed. The authors used a local measure to recalculate edge clustering coefficient every time when an edge is removed. Since, the measure is local, it can be calculated quickly and takes less execution time than that of Girvan and Newman's algorithm. The algorithm is based on short loops of edges (loops of length three) or triangles in the network. Edge clustering coefficient was defined based on these triangles. According to this algorithm, the edges between communities contain small edge clustering coefficient value. The edges with low values of clustering coefficients are iteratively removed during each iteration. Then, the clustering coefficient is recalculated again for the remaining edges in the network and the process continues. The main disadvantage of this algorithm is that it relies in the presence of triangles in the network. If real-world networks have few triangles, the algorithm fails to find correct communities. But, many of the real-world networks have a high proportion of triangles. Particularly, in social network, this type of triangles are more likely to occur (a friend of friend is one's friend). Therefore, this algorithm performs well in social network, but less well for other types of networks. The important problems in community detection algorithms are:

1. How to know that the produced communities by an algorithm are good ones?

2. Whether the community reveals the correct structure?

There should be some methods to say that the communities produced from the algorithm are the best communities for a given network. Newman and Girvan (2004) proposed an alternative approach based on the modularity as an *a posteriori* measure of the overall quality of a graph partition to solve the above said problems. Modularity measures internal connectivity, with reference to a randomized null model. The modularity is a numerical index of how good a particular division is and has been very influential in community detection literature. The value of modularity is high for good community divisions and low for poor ones. But, the time complexity remains high in this algorithm similar to that of GN algorithm. Hence, it is applied to small scale networks only.

To overcome the high time complexity of the algorithms designed by Girvan and Newman (2002) and Newman and Girvan (2004), Newman (2004) developed a fast algorithm, so as to suit for the networks those contain millions of nodes. Newman's fast algorithm is an agglomerative hierarchical clustering that starts with a state in which each node is a single community. Then, it repeatedly merges pairs of communities together, based on modularity which is a replacement to edge-betweenness centrality. The modularity is the measure of a cluster against the same cluster in a null, or random, graph and could be described as the notion that communities do not occur by random change. From then, several authors presented various approaches to optimize the algorithm proposed by Newman (2004). Algorithms that aim to maximize the modularity use techniques like spectral clustering and external optimization.

Exact modularity optimization is a problem that is computationally hard. Hence, approximation algorithms are necessary when dealing with large networks. Based on Newman's approach, Clauset et al. (2004) developed a new agglomerative method and applied stacks to refresh the values to optimize the modularity. The algorithm used the same greedy optimization technique, but, exploits shortcuts in the optimization problem and use more sophisticated data structures. This algorithm recurrently merged communities that optimize the production of modularity. The algorithm used max-heaps for sparse matrices instead of adjacency matrix. The authors pointed out that the update of the matrix used in Newman's (2004) algorithm involves a large number of useless operations, because the adjacency matrix is sparse in nature. Therefore, the same operations can be performed more efficiently by using max-heaps as data structure for sparse matrices that rearrange the data in the form of binary trees.

In the algorithm designed by Clauset et al. (2004), the data was arranged in the form of binary trees using max-heaps and the optimization of modularity was carried out using three data structures: matrix of modularity variations, max-heaps containing largest element of each row of the matrix, a simple array whose elements are the sums of the elements of each row of old matrix. This approach minimized the time taken for updates than that of Newman's algorithm and proved to be efficient for very large networks. Moreover, the algorithm produces a higher value of modularity. Unfortunately, this greedy algorithm has a tendency to produce giant communities that contain a large fraction of the nodes, even on synthetic networks that have no significant community structure. Moreover, it also slows down the algorithm considerably and makes it inapplicable to networks of more than a million nodes.

Clauset (2005) used a local measurement of community structure called local modularity and proposed an agglomerative algorithm to maximize the local modularity of the communities detected. Clauset et al. (2008) proposed a greedy hierarchical agglomerative algorithm which starts from each vertex being in a community and then consecutively joins two communities as the algorithm progresses. The whole process can be represented by a dendrogram. Newman (2006b) optimized the modularity using the modularity matrix and eigen values.

Baumes et al. (2004) described models and efficient algorithms for detecting groups (communities) functioning in communication networks which attempt to hide their functionality i.e. hidden groups. In the algorithm, communication networks were viewed as random graphs where the nodes are actors of the network and an edge represents a communication between the corresponding actors. The authors assumed that an approach to detect hidden groups should not rely on the semantic information contained in the communications since it is usually encrypted or unavailable. The authors pointed out that hidden group communication arises out of necessity and certainly non-random in behaviour. In order to identify the presence of a hidden group and its members, the authors used three notions namely internally connected, externally connected and disconnected. A group is said to be internally or externally connected if a message can be passed between any two group members without or with the use of outside third parties (in graph terminology it is connected graph or subgraph). A group is disconnected if it is not externally connected.

Blondel et al. (2008) used Louvin method which is a greedy optimization method that attempts to optimize the modularity of a partition of the network. The optimization is performed in two steps. First, the method looks for small communities by optimizing modularity locally. Second, it aggregates nodes belonging to the same community and builds a new network whose nodes are the communities. These steps are repeated iteratively until a maximum of modularity is attained and a hierarchy of communities is produced. In the first phase, a different community is assigned to each node of the network which leads to as many communities as there are nodes. Considering a node as i and its neighbour nodes as j, for each node i the neighbours of that node j are considered for evaluating the gain of modularity that would take place by placing the node i in the community of its neighbour j. The node i is then placed in one of the communities for which the gain has maximum value, if only this gain is positive. If no positive gain is possible, the node i remains in its original community itself. This process is applied repeatedly and sequentially for all nodes until no further improvement can be achieved.

The second phase of the algorithm builds a new network whose nodes are the communities found during the first phase. In this phase, weights of the links between the new nodes are given by the sum of the weight of the links between nodes in the corresponding two communities. Then, the first phase of the algorithm is reapplied to the resulting weighted network and iteration continues. The algorithm naturally incorporates the notion of hierarchy, as communities of communities are built during the process. As iteration progresses, the number of meta-communities decreases at each time step, until there are no more changes and a local maximum is attained. The algorithm is easy to implement and extremely fast due to the easy computation of modularity gains. The number of communities decreases drastically after a few iterations so that most of the running time is concentrated on the first iteration and the algorithm is also unaffected by the resolution limit problem of modularity.

The idea behind Random Walk is that the walk tends to be trapped in dense parts of a network corresponding to communities. Markov Cluster Algorithm (MCL) proposed by Van Dongen (2000) for weighted graphs uses random walks to simulate a flow on a graph which can be considered as a Markov chain. MCL uses the process of expansion and inflation in the input network until the convergence of the partition is achieved. Expansion raises the transfer matrix to a power which results in a matrix showing the probability for a random walker to start from node i and reach node j in certain number of steps. At each iteration, an inflation operator is used to strengthen the degree of connectivity of densely linked nodes and weaken the region of sparse connections. Inflation operator greatly influences the granularity of clusters. Pons and Latapy (2006) introduced a distance measure between vertices based on random walks. The distance is calculated from the probabilities that the random walker moves from a vertex to another in a fixed number of steps.

The idea of propagating labels through a network has been studied by Bagrow and Bollt (2005) in the *L-shell* method. In this technique, starting from a node with a label, the algorithm propagates the label step by step and includes more neighbour nodes until the end of a community is reached. The threshold value which is defined as the ratio of the number of edges inside and outside the community identifies the boundaries of the community.

The similar concept has been studied by Costa (Costa et al. 2004). Raghavan et al. (2007) proposed a label propagation algorithm for community detection in large networks. The algorithm is mainly appreciated for its near-linear time complexity. Unnecessary updates during every iteration of the algorithm increases the execution time in extremely large networks. To avoid unnecessary updates during each iteration, Xie and Szymanski (2011a) proposed an algorithm that updates label based on certain criteria by bookkeeping the information about the boundaries of the currently existing communities. Xie and Szymanski (2013a) stabilized the label propagation dynamics by introducing a set of operators to control the propagation process.

3.2. Overlapping Community Detection

A very important property for community discovery is the ability to return an overlapping coverage i.e. the possibility of a node to be part of more than one community. The presence of nodes in two or more communities is hard to manage with classical graph clustering methods where every vertex of the graph belongs to exactly only one community. Hence, community detection algorithms must allow and detect, overlapping groups. Forcing a node in a network into a single community and not allowing for overlap could prevent the detection of the true underlying community structures (Palla et al. 2005; Lancichinetti and Fortunato 2009b).

Most of the literature on community detection focuses on the disjoint community identification techniques. The study of overlapping communities has received muchattention in the last years. Overlapping communities have numerous applications and is very attractive for researchers. Hence, in recent years, great advances have been made in the field of overlapping community detection.

Nodes belonging to several communities arises naturally from real data (Palla et al. 2005). Considering one's own personal network, one will naturally belong to several communities like family, co-workers and friends. The concept of overlap occurs in social networks, biological networks and so on. Particularly, social networks are naturally characterized by multiple community memberships. For example, in online social networks, one person joins unlimited hobby groups and simultaneously associate with as many groups as he/she wishes; a researcherbelongs to multiple research groups in academic network. Studies about overlap shows, it is indeed a significant feature of many real-world social networks.

Detecting overlapping nodes and communities is a crucial task in understanding and analyzing the social network structures. If hierarchical algorithms are applied to social networks where individuals associate across many social groups, then, it may miss the important information about an individual's concurrent interaction with the numerous social circles. This reason has been the intuitive justification for designing overlapping community detection algorithms.

In this section some of the familiar overlapping community detection algorithms particularly in the perspective of social networks are discussed. Overlapping community detection algorithms has been reviewed and categorized into five classes (Xie et al. 2013b) namely Clique Percolation algorithms (CPM), Agent based algorithms, Fuzzy based algorithms, Local expansion and Optimization algorithms and Line graph and Link partitioning algorithms.

3.2.1. *Clique Percolation*

In the mathematical area of graph theory, a *clique* in an undirected graph is a subset of its vertices such that every two vertices in the subset are connected by an edge. In the social sciences, a clique is a group of persons who interact with each other more regularly and intensely than others in the same setting. Cliques have also been studied in computer science: the task of finding whether there is a clique of a given size in a graph. The first work on detecting overlapping communities using Clique Percolation algorithm (CPM) started with Palla et al. (2005). The author extended the Girvan Newman's problem to find overlapping communities where each node can belong to one or more communities. Since then, a very large amount of algorithms have been proposed with great improvements in time and efficiency.

The basic assumption of CPM is that the internal edges of a community are likely to form cliques due to their high density. The author used the term k-clique to indicate a complete graph with k vertices. Two k -cliques are adjacent if they share $k-1$ vertices. The connected components in the resultant graph identify which cliques compose the communities. Overlap between communities is possible; since a vertex can be in multiple *k-cliques* simultaneously. as shown in Figure 3.1 (overlapping vertices are shown by the bigger dots). CPM assumes that the graph has large number of cliques and it is suitable only for networks with dense connected parts. If a graph contains few cliques, then it fails to detect meaningful covers. A software package to detect overlapping communities on biological networks implementing the CPM called CFinder was designed by Palla and coworkers (Adamcsek et al. 2006).

Ignoring the possible directionality of the links during the analysis of a network is the important limitation of CPM. The direction of a single link in most real network denotes either flow of information or the asymmetry of the relation between the nodes. Palla et al. (2007a) considered the directionality of links and proposed a simple measure for the nodes within the modules to characterize their roles in terms of the numbers of their incoming and outgoing links. The author defined the notion of directed k-cliques and proposed a restricted version of CPM for directed networks, denoted as Clique Percolation Method with directed cliques (CPMd), in which only directed k-cliques can be used for the identification of modules. Directed k-cliques are defined as complete subgraphs of size k in which an ordering can be made such that between any pair of nodes there is a directed link pointing from the node with the higher order towards the lower one.

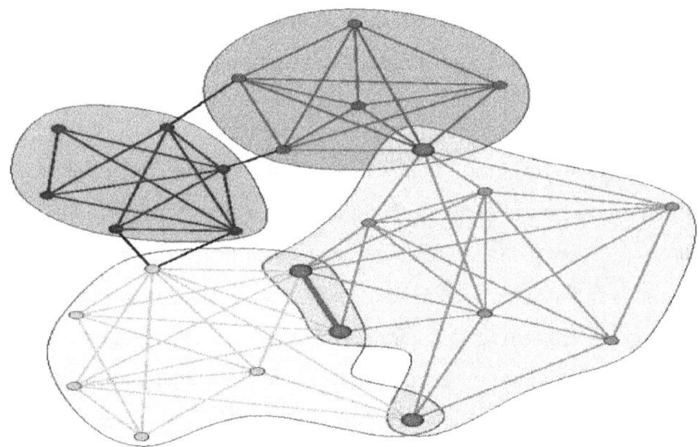

Figure 3.1: K-clique Communities (Palla et al. 2005)

While analyzing the network properties, if link weights are considered it provides a deeper understanding about the overlapping structure of real-world networks. In weighted networks, the CPM removes the links that are below a fixed weight threshold (W) and consider the remaining connections as unweighted to search for modules. Clique Percolation Method with weights (CPMw) introduced by Farkas et al. (2007) is an extension of unweighted CPM that takes into account the link weights by incorporating the subgraph intensity examined by Onnela et al. (2005) into the search algorithm. The intensity of a subgraph is equal to the geometric mean of its link weights.

In the CPMw, a k-clique is included into a module only if it has intensity larger than a fixed threshold value. The most important difference between the CPM and CPMw is that all links included in a CPM module must have weights higher than the link weight threshold. However, the modules obtained by the CPMw often contain links weaker than the intensity threshold too. In a weighted network where strong links prefer to be neighbours, the above two algorithms provide similar results. Results from the CPM and the CPMw differ strongly for graphs where strong links prefer to have weak links as neighbours, i.e. links are disassortative with respect to their weights. When compared with CPM, it produces modules with *smoother* contours with a particular intensity threshold. It expands slightly the modules located by the CPM and may attach to each module additional k-cliques containing weaker links.

Real-world complex networks may consist of nodes that belong to more than one community and the communities may be further divided hierarchically (Palla et al. 2007b; Sales-Pardo et al. 2007). The hierarchical community detection algorithms explore the hierarchical structure but not the overlaps between communities. Overlapping community detection algorithms may uncover overlapping community structure of networks, but may be incapable of finding the hierarchy of communities.

Shen et al. (2009a) proposed EAGLE (agglomerativE hierarchicAl clusterinG based on maximaL cliquE) to uncover both hierarchical and overlapping community structure of networks. The algorithm EAGLE deals with the set of maximal cliques rather than the set of sole vertices and uses agglomerative framework. A maximal clique is a clique which is not a subset of any other cliques. In the first part of the algorithm, all the maximal cliques in the network are found. If the maximal cliques are from some other larger maximal cliques (called as subordinate maximal cliques) then it is discarded using a threshold value. Each subordinate vertex is also taken as an initial community comprising the sole vertex and the similarity between each pair of communities are calculated. Then the pair of communities with the maximum similarity are selected and incorporated into a new one and again the similarity between the new community and other communities are calculated repeatedly till only one community remains. In the second stage of the algorithm, the optimal cut on the dendrogram is determined by the extended modularity with a weight based on the number of overlapping memberships and obtain a hierarchy of overlapping communities which reveals the community structure of network more completely. The algorithm is computationally expensive.

Kumpula et al. (2008) presented a fast community detection algorithm called Sequential Clique Percolation method (SCP) for weighted and unweighted networks for cliques of a chosen size. It sequentially inserts links to the network and keeps track of the emerging community structure. When links are inserted in order of decreasing weight, the algorithm detects *k-clique* communities at chosen threshold levels in a single run and simultaneously produces a dendrogram representation of hierarchical community structure. This algorithm has been specifically designed for dense weighted networks containing hierarchical communities where weight-based thresholding of either the links or the cliques formed by them is necessary for obtaining meaningful information on the structure. The computational time of the SCP algorithm scales linearly with the number of k-cliques in the network. SCP is faster than CPM and allows multiple weight thresholds in a single run.

3.2.2. Link Based Algorithms

The idea of partitioning links instead of nodes to discover community structure has also been explored. In this type of algorithms, a node in the original network is called overlapping if links connected to it are put in more than one group. Ahn (Ahn et al. 2010) approached communities as groups of links rather than nodes and showed that this approach successfully identified overlapping communities and its hierarchy. Instead of assuming that a community is a set of nodes with many links between them, the authors considered a community to be a set of closely interrelated links and used a hierarchical clustering with a similarity between links to build a dendrogram where each leaf is a link from the original network and branches represent link communities. By cutting the dendrogram at various thresholds, link communities were extracted at multiple levels. Each node inherits all memberships of its links and can belong to multiple overlapping communities. The link dendrogram provides a rich hierarchy of structure if the best level to cut the tree is properly determined.

The algorithm proposed by Rosvall (2008) used map equation method to decompose a network into modules by optimally compressing a description of information flows on the network. The result of the decomposition is a map that both simplifies and highlights the regularities in the network structure and their relationships. In this algorithm, modules which compose the network were identified by finding an optimally compressed description of how information flows on the network through random walks. Evans (Evans et al. 2010) extended line graph to clique graph where cliques of a given order are represented as node in a weighted graph. Fortunato (2010) suggested that there is no guarantee that link graph provides higher quality community detection than node based community detection.

3.2.3. Fuzzy

In non-fuzzy overlapping, each vertex belongs to one or more communities with equal strength: an individual either belongs to a community or it does not. With fuzzy overlapping, each individual may also belong to more than one community but the strength of its membership to each community can vary. Gregory (2011) expressed memberships as a belonging coefficient that describes how a given node is distributed between communities. Zhang et al. (2007) developed a method combining spectral mapping, fuzzy clustering and optimization of a quality function. It converts a network to $(k\text{-}1)$ dimensional Euclidean space and use the fuzzy c-means algorithm to detect up to k communities. The method showed how detection accuracy and computational efficiency rely on the user specified value k which is the upper bound on the number of communities.

The approach designed by Nepusz et al. (2008) allows each vertex of the graph to belong to multiple communities at the same time, determined by exact numerical membership degrees, even in the presence of uncertainty in the data being analyzed. In this algorithm, first the optimal membership degrees are calculated with respect to a given goal function. Then, based on the membership degrees, a new measure identifies outlier vertices that do not belong to any of the communities, bridge vertices that belong significantly to more than one single community and regular vertices that fundamentally restrict their interactions within their own community, while also being able to quantify the centrality of a vertex with respect to its dominant community. The number of communities for this algorithm can be given in advance or determined by the algorithm itself using a fuzzy variant of the modularity function.

The technique is able to discover the fuzzy community structure of different real-world networks including but, not limited to social networks and scientific collaboration networks with high confidence and can also be used for prediction in case of uncertainty in the dataset analyzed. This algorithm is expected to be highly useful in the analysis of relatively small datasets (up to the magnitude of a thousand vertices), because it assumes that every vertex has the possibility to connect to all other vertices. This algorithm is not suitable for very large networks, since it is not possible that all vertices are connected to all other vertices.

Wang et al.(2009) combined disjoint detection methods with local optimization algorithms. First, a partition is obtained from any algorithm for disjoint community detection. Then, communities attempt to add or remove nodes. Variance, the difference of two fitness scores on a community, either including a node or removing node, is computed. The normalized variances form a fuzzy membership vector of the node. Wang et al. (2012) used clique optimization to identify granular overlaps and fuzzy detection to identify modular overlaps and proposed a dynamic community evolution technique. But, this algorithm is suitable for dynamic networks and not intended for static networks.

Psorakis (Psorakis et al. 2011) have identified a probabilistic approach to community detection that utilizes a Bayesian non-negative matrix factorization (NMF) model to extract overlapping modules from a network. This algorithm uses a generative model in a probabilistic framework in which priors exist over the model parameters. The number of latent communities (or classes of nodes) is used as model order selection in this framework. The authors showed that the degree of participation of two individuals in various communities is a latent generator of the expected number of interactions between them. The algorithm demonstrated how NMF not only captures the membership of a node in multiple communities, but also quantifies how strongly that individual participates in each of the groups. By using the entropy of the node membership distribution, core nodes in each community or inversely, broker nodes that act as mediators between different groups were identified. The authors emphasized that the mean entropy of the membership distributions can help to quantify the degree of fuzziness in the network or the clarity of community structure. The limitation of NMF is, it assumes a fully observed adjacency matrix which is not applicable to many real-world networks.

3.2.4. Local Expansion and Optimization

Algorithms that depend on local expansion and optimization method rely on a local benefit function that characterizes the quality of a densely connected group of nodes. Gregory S (2007) proposed a Cluster-Overlap Newman Girvan Algorithm (CONGA) which is an "overlapping" version of existing disjoint community detection algorithm. CONGA extends Girvan and Newman's GN algorithm, by splitting a vertex into two vertices repeatedly during the divisive clustering process.

CONGA considers both split betweenness, defined by the number of shortest paths on the imaginary edge and also the conventional edge betweenness. In this algorithm, first edge betweenness of edges and split betweenness of vertices are calculated and the edge with maximum edge betweenness is removed.It also splits vertex with maximum split betweenness. Then, edge betweenness and split betweenness are calculated again and the process of edge removal or vertex splitting is repeated until no edges remain. In CONGA, a network is initially treated as a single community. As iteration progresses, network is split into communities repeatedly until only singleton communities remain. The speed of the algorithm depends on the number of vertices that are split and on how easily the network breaks into separate components.

Baumes et al. (2005b) iteratively improved the candidate cluster of CONGA by a two phase method where a network is first broken into a number of disjoint *seed* communities and then adding vertices to and removing vertices from the candidate set until its density is maximized. It depends on finding a local maximum of density. The authors adopted the same notions formulated by Baumas et al. (2004), i.e. a group in a social network forms a community if its communication *density* function achieves a local maximum in the collection of groups that are *close* to that group. Two groups were called close if they become identical by changing the membership of just one actor and added one more notion: the density of a group is defined as the average density of the communication exchanges between the actors of the group. Thus, a group is a community if any new member is added to it or any current member removed from it. Using these strategies, a new efficient algorithm for initializing the seed clusters and performing the iterative improvement through a procedure List Aggregate (LA) for initializing the clusters and a procedure Iterative Scan (IS) which iteratively improves any given set of clusters was designed. The combined algorithm identified overlapping subgraphs in a general graph and provided significant improvement over the former algorithm (Baumes et al. 2004) and produced clusters of better quality.

A revised version of CONGA (Gregory 2008) named CONGO (CONGA Optimized) has been developed by Gregory (2009) that uses local betweenness to optimize the speed. In CONGO, edge betweenness and split betweenness are calculated by counting the number of shortpaths. The short paths are no longer than h (a parameter of the algorithm). It is especially effective in discovering small-diameter communities in large networks. The author also proposed a new transformation algorithm named Peacock which uses two phases for detecting overlapping communities. The transformation and the processing of the algorithm are as follows:

- Calculate the split betweenness of all vertices.
- Choose the vertex with the maximum split betweenness. Split it into two, according to its best split.
- Recalculate the split betweenness of vertices.
- Repeat from step 2 until the maximum split betweenness is sufficiently small.
- For each split vertex, place a new edge between the two resulting vertices.

The above mentioned approach has the potential to convert any disjoint community detection algorithm into an overlapping community detection algorithm.

To provide exhaustive information about the modular structure of a graph, both overlapping communities and hierarchies between them should be identified by an algorithm. Lancichinetti et al. (2009c) proposed a method based on the local optimization of the fitness function which finds both overlapping communities and the hierarchical structure in the communities. In the proposed method, the communities are treated as local structures, involving the nodes belonging to the modules themselves plus at most an extended neighbourhood of them. So, it performs a local exploration of the network searching for the natural community of each node. Several visits may happen to one node which places the node in more than one community. The node is distributed to different communities after finding the highest fitness value through local optimization, thus overlapping communities are naturally identified. The size of each community is decided by tuning the resolution parameter which leads to meaningful hierarchical communities. The computational complexity of the algorithm depends on the size of the communities and the extent of their overlaps, which in turn strongly depends on the specific network being studied along with the value of the resolution parameter. The only difference between this algorithm and that of Baumes et al. (2005b) is that a seed community is simply a vertex that is not yet assigned to any community. This algorithm provides a general framework that can be adapted by any community detection algorithm by choosing a different expression for the fitness function or a different optimization procedure of the fitness as a single cluster.

Goldberg et al. (2010) formulated two simple properties, axioms, for a set of members to qualify as a community. The authors specified a set of guidelines for what should constitute a community. Two axioms namely *connectedness* and *local optimality* were used in the algorithm. Connected Iterative scan (CIS) is a modification of Iterative Scan (IS) proposed by Baumes et al. (2005b). Connectedness denotes that a community should induce a connected subgraph in the network. If the only path one node to another in the community is through an external node, then the community is incomplete. According to the axiom local optimality, the density of a community cannot be improved with the removal or addition of a single node. CIS performs a number of scans repeatedly for a set until no change in the set occurs, after which the set is declared to be a community. The scan is performed in the order of increasing node degree for all nodes. When the scanning process is completed, the connectivity of the set is examined and if it consists of multiple connected components, it is replaced by connected component with the highest density. Then the next scan is started. In addition to local optimality introduced by Baumes et al. (2005a and 2005b), this algorithm used connected property. Since it is not easy to identify all communities satisfying these properties, a simple heuristic has been used to identify overlap between communities. From the various experiments conducted through the algorithm, the authors showed that in many social networks there are sets that satisfy the above said axioms. The disadvantage of this algorithm is it may produce a large number of highly overlapping communities which can be managed by effective post processing and merging the highly similar communities.

A connection based algorithm DOCA (Detecting Overlapping Community Algorithm) algorithm has been presented by Nguyen et al. (2011). DOCA consists of three main procedures. In the first phase, to group a set of nodes in a local community, its internal density is calculated. The internal density should satisfy the connectedness function. The function solely depends only on the size of local communities, and so it can be locally computed and adapted to multiple communities of different sizes. In this phase, tiny communities of sizes less than four may be left unlabeled because of the size constraint. These unlabeled nodes are revisited again in the third phase. After the first phase, the raw network community structures that are dense parts of the network together with outliers are identified in bottom up manner. As some of those dense parts can possibly share significant common substructures, it should be merged in the second phase. After the completion of these two phases, some nodes or edges may still exist due to their less attraction to the rest of the network. The nodes that are left unlabeled in the first phase are revisited again to group them into appropriate communities or classify them as outliers based on their connectivity structures. DOCA requires just local knowledge about network topology and requires only very limited parameters.

Order Statistics and Local Optimization method (OSLAM) is the first algorithm capable to detect clusters accounting for edge directions, edge weights, overlapping communities, hierarchy and community dynamics (Lancichinetti et al. 2011). It is a method that optimizes locally the statistical significance of clusters defined with respect to a global null model (Lancichinetti et al. 2010; Radicchi et al. 2010). OSLAM uses significance as a fitness measure in order to evaluate the clusters. It consists of three phases

- First it looks for significant clusters until convergence.
- Then it analyzes the resulting set of clusters, trying to detect their internal structure or possible unions thereof.
- Finally, it detects the hierarchical structure of the clusters.

The main features of OSLAM are: significant clusters, cluster hierarchy, identification of homeless vertices, easy generalization to handle directed and weighted graphs and overlapping communities. The algorithm is particularly superior on directed graphs and in the detection of strongly overlapping communities. It efficiently recognizes the absence of community structure or the presence of randomness in graphs. The limitation of this algorithm is it performs lot of iterations, to get more accurate results, which increases the complexity of the algorithm.

Padrol-Sureda et al. (2010) developed Overlapping Community Search (OCA) based on the idea of mapping each node to a high dimensional vector space. Each subset of nodes is defined as the sum of individual vectors in the set. The fitness function is defined as the directed Laplacian on a function which is the squared Euclidean length of a subset vector. OCA starts with a random neighbourhood of the seed and using a greedy approach adds(removes) the node whose additions(removal) to the set implies the greatest increment of the fitness function. The process continues until a local maximum is found. The main objective of this algorithm is the optimization of a new fitness function for evaluating the quality of the communities.

3.2.5. Agent and Dynamic based Algorithms

Label propagation is an agent based iterative method where labels are passed between the members of a (partially) labeled set of data points. Raghavan et al. (2007) proposed a Label Propagation Algorithm (LPA) for community detection in large networks to detect disjoint communities. LPA was extended by Gregory (2010), by modifying the nodes to possess multiple labels called Community Overlap Label PRopagation Algorithm (COPRA). COPRA keeps the good computational performance of LPA and is able to give good results in many cases. In order to determine how the node spreads its information to others and to process the information received from other nodes in dynamic process, Xie et al. (2011b)proposed a Speaker-Listener Label Propagation Algorithm (SLPA) to mimic people's preference of spreading most frequently discussed opinions.

Chen et al. (2010b) introduced a game-theoretic framework to detect overlapping communities. The formation of communities is interpreted as a community formation game played by selfish agents on the social network. Each agent has an intrinsic utility that associates with the communities it joins and those it does not. Individuals in social network only aim to maximize their own utility. The formation of communities is the joint result of each agent's selfish decision. A community structure can be interpreted as Nash equilibrium of this game. The authors formulate the agents' utility by the combination of a gain function and a loss function to match the real world scenario where each individual not only receives benefit from the communities the agents belongs to but also needs to pay certain cost to maintain the membership in the communities. Each agent can select multiple communities which naturally capture the concept of overlapping communities. The gain function works on Newman's modularity function and a simple loss function that reflects the intrinsic costs incurred when people join the communities. The author suggested that better gain and loss functions can be derived by deeper understanding of the community formation process in real world.

Cazabet et al. (2010) identified an agent based approach to detect overlapping communities. The author formulated two new concepts called intrinsic communities and longitudinal detection to study the evolution of communities. But, this approach was designed only for dynamic networks. Liu et al. (2010) used ant colony based algorithms which uses virtual ants to detect communities within a collection of email objects. The swarm portion on the algorithm creates a number of virtual ants that wonder over a grid deciding whether or not to pick up an email object. The email objects that are picked up are dropped in piles of similar objects. The email objects are randomly distributed on a grid and then virtual ants are allowed to randomly walk the grid evaluating the objects.

Bradley and Keith (2013) recommended a unique agent based approach to community detection that combines the individual's view of a community, not having the view the graph as a whole. The author used swarm intelligence as a means of removing the central control mechanism. The unique approach uses each individual's view of the communities, called friendship groups to allow network to be analyzed in smaller pieces. In this algorithm first friendship groups are detected and assigned a unique identifier and non-propagating nodes within each friendship group are found after which the assigned friendship-group identifiers are propagated. This algorithm use distributed agents that operate autonomously and have decentralized control.

3.3.   Summary

Many algorithms have been developed from various disciplines such as physics, biology, applied mathematics, computer and social sciences. But, the question of which algorithm suits best for which application is still a question of research. In spite of variety of algorithms available in the community detection research, there is still no universal agreement on what a network with communities should look like. Based on the different views of various researchers, many community detection algorithms have been designed. In general, community detection can be classified into two categories: disjoint and overlapping. Vast number of algorithms exists in the literature to detect disjoint communities. In complex networks, communities may overlap. Particularly, in social networks, overlapping occurs in social circles such as workplace, social clubs, religious groups etc. There are few algorithms designed to identify overlapping community structures. In this chapter an overview of various community detection algorithms that aims to detect disjoint or overlapping communities were discussed.

CHAPTER IV

BENCHMARKS AND METRICS

Depending on the structure of the network, community detection algorithms can be classified as disjoint and overlapping. Numerous algorithms have been proposed for detecting both disjoint and overlapping communities on static networks and dynamic network. A detailed list of most popular disjoint and overlapping community detection algorithms designed for static networks are listed in this chapter.

4.1. Benchmarks

The major issues that arises in the problem of community detection are:

- How to test the algorithms?
- How to know that the communities found by the algorithms are the correct ones?

Synthetic networks and real-world networks solves the above mentioned issues. Any algorithm that aims to detect communities from complex networks should be tested either with real-world networks or artificial networks or both. Real-networks are formed by observing a social community and representing it in the form of network structure. Artificial networks are generated by algorithms that are designed to produce a network similar to that of real-world network. Synthetic networks are examples of artificial network. Since synthetic networks are artificially generated its ground-truth is known. The ground truth values of the generated network shows the actual communities to be expected from the network.

There are several limitations for why the real world networks alone are not considered for testing the algorithms. The first limitation is lack of such huge networks. Second, the network is characterized by topological properties like average degree, degree distributions, shortest path etc. It becomes tedious to control these topological properties in a real world network. Moreover, the algorithm can be tested on a specific and limited set of features alone. The solution to the second and third question is evaluation metrics. An evaluation metric is used to evaluate the output of the algorithm.

4.1.1. Real-world Networks

Though there are numerous real-world networks to check the algorithms, few networks are very commonly used by many of the researchers. The networks which are popularly used for testing are listed in this section. Zachary (1977) Karate Club is one of the classic studies in social network analysis. In this study, Zachary observed social interactions between members of a karate club in American university over a period of two years and build a network of connections with 34 vertices and 78 edges among members of the club based on the social interactions. During the course of the study, a disagreement developed between the administrator of the club and the club's instructor. As a result, the club split into two smaller communities with the administrator and the teacher being the central persons accordingly.

American college football network represents the schedule of Division I games for the 2000 season. It consists of 115 vertices and 616 edges which are the representations of football teams and regular season games among them respectively. During the season, all of the 115 teams are divided into 12 conferences containing around 8 to 12 teams each. Games are more frequent between members of the same conference than between members of different conferences. Each conference can be considered as a community.

The concept of social network does not limit to humans, but can be for group of animals. A famous social network of animals described by Luessue (Luessue et al. 2003), is a network of social relationships or associations among dolphins. In this network, nodes are dolphins and links express some kind of relationships among them. For example, they belong to the same family or they have been observed together. The author observed 62 dolphins living off doubtful sound. Two dolphins are connected if they have been seen swimming together.

4.1.2. Synthetic Networks

Artificial networks are easy to generate, while controlling their properties is also easy. If there is a model that is able to generate an artificial network with features similar to those of real-world networks, then it can be seen as a complement to real world network, but not as a substitute of real world network. It is necessary to have good benchmarks for studying the behavior of a proposed community detection algorithm and to compare the performance across various algorithms. In order to accurately perform these two analyses, networks in which the ground truth is known are needed. The real-world networks, which are often collected from online or observed interactions, do not give a clear enough picture due to their lack of "ground truth". Though synthetic networks contain few important features of real-world networks, they are commonly used by researchers in the community detection field to test their algorithms.

There are several kinds of synthetic benchmarks proposed by researchers to test their algorithms (Radichi et al. 2004; Duch et al. 2005). The most famous bench marks for community detection are GN Benchmarks and LFR (Lancichinetti-Fortunato-Radicchi) benchmarks.

GN Benchmarks

This benchmark is a class of networks introduced by Girvan and Newman (2002) with 128 nodes, divided into 4 groups with 32 nodes each. The GN bench mark was a network of a reasonable size when it was introduced. This benchmark was widely used by various researchers for testing their algorithms (Danon *et al.* 2005). Most community detection algorithms perform very well on the GN benchmark due to the simplicity of its structure. But, there exists some drawbacks of GN benchmarks such as: The average degree of the network is same (following a Poisson distribution) and all communities have the same size. These limitations make this benchmark unsuitable for complex networks which are known to be characterized by heterogeneous distributions (Newman 2003; Boccaletti et al. 2006) of degree and community sizes (Guimera et al. 2003; Palla et al. 2005). In order to overcome these limitation Lancichinetti et al. (2008 and 2009) proposed LFR benchmarks for disjoint and overlapping communities.

LFR Benchmarks

Due to the availability of millions of nodes in real world networks and heterogeneous distribution of node degrees which obey power law distribution, the researchers started to develop benchmarks to tackle the large scale networks. Among the various benchmarks available in the literature, the LFR benchmark exhibits the realistic properties of actual networks with controlled power law degree and community size distributions. It is a generalization of the benchmark of Newman and Girvan which is a random graph with a more realistic community structure as the vertex degrees as well as the community sizes have a power-law distribution. Lancichinetti and Fortunato (2009b) applied this benchmark to assess the clustering quality of different graph clustering methods including algorithms that are based on modularity maximization and algorithms based on other approaches.

In most real-world networks representing interaction data, there are a few nodes with high degree and many nodes with low degree; with a smooth transition in between i.e. the degree distribution is heavy-tailed (Barabasi et al. 2009; Clauset et al, 2009). A realistic generative model should be able to reproduce this type of degree distribution. In LFR networks, node degrees and community sizes are both power-law distributed. LFR Benchmarks are a class of graphs with planted community structure and heterogeneous degree distributions. The planted *l-partition* model is a class of graphs whose vertices are divided into *l* equal-sized groups, such that the probability that two vertices of the same group are linked is p, while the probability that two vertices of different groups are linked is q, with $p > q$. A network is generated based on a user specified set of parameters related to network size, node degree range and community size. LFR benchmarks use these parameters to construct a suitable set of communities around which the network is constructed.

The LFR model brings benchmarks closer to the features observed in real-world networks. LFR benchmarks, presents a much harder test to algorithms and makes it easier to disclose their limits. Moreover, the LFR benchmark graphs can be built very quickly, i.e., the complexity of the construction process is linear in the number of links of the graph. So, one can perform tests on very large systems, provided the method at study is fast enough to analyze them. Hence, it is widely used by the researchers to generate synthetic network with known ground truth values.

4.2. Metrics for Evaluation

After testing the algorithm using real-world networks or benchmark graphs, the next important task to be performed is evaluating the results of the output produced by the algorithm. The important question that arises here is: How to assess that the results of a community detection algorithms is better than another algorithm? In real-world complex networks, it is hard to know the actual communities that are hidden in the network. In order to find real communities, a proper quality function is essential.

A quality function is used to measure that evaluate the quality of results (communities) obtained by the community detection algorithm. A quality function is a function that assigns a number to each community of network and ranks the communities based on the quality function scores. Communities with high scores are said to be good communities. But determining which score is better or good depends upon the quality function adopted and on the specific concept of community to be detected i.e. whether it is disjoint community, overlapping community, evolving communities etc. Since the quality function depends on the specific type of community to be detected, there is no universally accepted definition of quality function. There exists various quality metrics for evaluating the various types of communities detected by algorithms.

4.2.1. Metrics for Real-world Networks

When evaluating communities produced by a community detection algorithm on real-world networks, there is usually no known correct solutions. Quality of solution must be assured in different ways using some evaluation metrics. There are number of evaluation metrics for real-world networks in the literature used by various algorithms to justify the output produced by them are correct. Important metrics for disjoint and overlapping communities are discussed in this section.

Metrics for Disjoint Communities

Modularity Q proposed by Newman and Girvan (2004) has been the best known and most used quality function and has been applied in many detection algorithms. Modularity measures the quality of a partition of a network into communities by comparing essentially the number of links inside a given community with the expected value for a randomized network of the same size and degrees. Modularity measure can be said as a comparison between observed density of edges within communities and expected density of edges within the same communities in random network. Modularity is applied to a network after all partitions are detected. The input to the modularity function is the network and its communities, and the output is a real number between -1 and 1. Let e_{ij} be the fraction of edges in the network that connect nodes in community i to those in community j, and a_i is the same expected fraction of edges within the same community z denoted as

$$a_i = \sum_j e_{ij}$$

The modularity Q defined by Newman and Girvan(2004) is expressed as

$$Q = \sum_{i \in U} (e_{ii} - a_i^2)$$

When the output of Q is high, then it denotes good communities. Modularity is always smaller than one, but it can be a negative value also when each node represents a single community. When the whole network is a single community, then the two terms are equal and cancels other which makes the modularity to become zero. Modularity values and their meaning are:

- If value of Q is close to 1 it indicates good community detection
- If value of Q is 0, it shows random partitioning, i.e., there is only one community in the network

Partitions of the network with maximum modularity are considered as best one or a very good one. Due to this feature, researchers who were interested in the community detection field attempted to maximize the modularity value using various techniques (Newman 2004; Blondel et al. 2008; Clauset et al. 2004; Danon et al. 2006). A large value for the modularity does not always mean that a graph have a community structure. Random graphs may have partitions with large modularity values (Guimera et al. 2004; Richard and Bornhold 2006), even though they do not exhibit community structure, due to the fluctuations in the distribution of edges in the graph. For example the distribution of edges among the nodes is highly homogeneous in Erdos-Renyi model. The degree of the node is binomial, so most nodes have equal or similar degree and do not contain communities. Some of the drawbacks of the above mentioned modularity are:

- It allows a node to be put in just one community at a time. Though it is possible to discover sub-communities, iteratively applying the algorithm to each of the partitions found, detecting partially overlapped communities is not possible. Real complex networks are never divided into sharp sub networks, particularly the networks formed from the social relationships and interactions usually nodes belong to multiple communities.
- It requires global knowledge of graph topology
- Many modularity optimization methods require a certain knowledge about the number of communities in the graph
- Resolution limits. It is shown in Fortunato and Barthelemy that modularity optimization may fail to identify communities smaller than a certain size and this induces a resolution limit on the community detected by a pure modularity optimization approach.
- Based on the modularity of Newman, various modifications of modularity have been done by researchers in various aspects such as modularity for weighted edges (Newman 2004), for directed graphs (Arenas et al. 2007), for bipartite graph (Guimera et al. 2007), for random graphs (Richard Borhold., 2007) and for overlapping graphs (Nicosia et al. 2007).

Metrics for Overlapping Communities

In order to make use of modularity for overlapping communities, an extension of modularity to evaluate the goodness of overlapped community decomposition was proposed by Nicosia (Nicosia et al. 2009). In overlapping communities, each node can belong to many communities with varying strength, which is in general not equal for all communities. Given a graph $G(E,V)$, Nicosia choose as null–model as a random graph corresponding to $G(E,V)$ where each node has an out degree and in degree as in the original graph, and where no particular community partition can be derived by structural properties of the graph, i.e. where the probability that a node z belongs to a given community c with a belonging factor $\alpha_{i,c}$ does not depend upon the probability that any other node j in the network does belong to the same community with $\alpha_{j,c}$. The expected belonging coefficient of any possible link $l_{i,j}$ starting from a node into community c is simply the average of all possible coefficients of belonging to c of z, is represented as

$$\beta^{out}_{l(i,j),c} = \frac{\sum_{j \in V} f(\alpha_{i,c}, \alpha_{j,c})}{|V|}$$

Accordingly, the expected belonging coefficient of any link pointing to a node going into community c is written as

$$\beta^{in}_{l(i,j),c} = \frac{\sum_{i \in V} f(\alpha_{i,c}, \alpha_{j,c})}{|V|}$$

The belonging coefficients shown in the above equations are used to weight the probability of having respectively, a link starting at node z and a link pointing to node j. The modularity for overlapped communities can be accordingly formulated as

$$Q_{ov} = \frac{1}{m} \sum_{c \hat{I} C} \sum_{i,j \hat{I} V} [\beta_{l(i,j),c} A_{ij} - \frac{\beta^{out}_{l(i,j),c} \kappa^{out}_i \beta^{in}_{l(i,j),c} \kappa^{in}_j}{m}]$$

The extension of the definition of modularity to the case of overlapping communities still depends on the choice of $f(\alpha_{i,c}, \alpha_{j,c})$, i.e., on the way one choose to weight the contribution of each edge to the modularity calculated for community c.

4.2.2. Metrics for Synthetic Networks

The advantage of using synthetic networks for testing the data is that the ground truth is known. Commonly used computer-generated benchmarks start with a network of well-defined communities. Then, this structure is degraded by rewiring or removing links and it gets harder and harder for the algorithms to detect the original partition. At the end, the network reaches a point where it is essentially random. This kind of benchmark may be called as *open*. The performance on these benchmarks is evaluated by various similarity measures. In order to compare the partitions delivered by the algorithm and the built in modular structure of a benchmark, several similarity measurements were designed. The similarity measure compares the solution obtained by an algorithm with the original community structure, evaluating the similarity of both partitions.

Metrics for Disjoint Communities

For disjoint community detection, a number of measures have been proposed for comparing identified partitions with the known partitions (Danon et al. 2005; Leskovec et al. 2010). Two most widely used measures are the Normalized Mutual Information (NMI) and Omega Index. NMI is a commonly used in the context of classic cluster analysis, to compare two different partitions of the same data set. NMI is based on mutual information, i.e., it is used to measure the amount of mutual information between two divisions. If the mutual information is shared with true communities, the better the clustering is. NMI employs the nodes label information and evaluates the performance of community detection algorithm. It is the widely used similarity measurement which is based on information theory. NMI is commonly used for evaluating the disjoint communities.

Metrics for Overlapping Communities

For comparing the known communities and computer disjoint communities, there are various standard measures. But only few of them are suitable for overlapping communities. An commonly used measure is a variant of normalized mutual information. The extension of NMI for overlapping clustering suggested by Lancichinetti et al. (2007) is used in this work to evaluate the output generated by the algorithm. For overlapping communities, NMI measures the fraction of nodes in agreement between two covers. For two random variables X,Y the mutual information is calculated as

$$NMI(X/Y) = 1 - \frac{1}{2}(H(X/Y)_{norm} + H(Y/X)_{norm})$$

$$H(X/Y)_{norm} = \frac{1}{|C_X|} \sum_k \frac{\min_{l \in (1, 2, \dots | CY)} H(X_K / Y_l)}{H(X_k)}$$

$$H(Y/X)_{norm} = \frac{1}{|C_Y|} \sum_k \frac{\min_{l \in (1, 2, \dots | CX)} H(Y_K / X_l)}{H(Y_k)}$$

Where $H(X/Y)$ and $H(Y/X)$ are conditional entropy, $|C_X|$ and $|C_Y|$ are the number of clusters in X and Y respectively. The NMI is computed in two steps. First, the pair of clusters that are more to each other in two clustering are found. Then, the average of the mutual information between those pairs of clusters is calculated. The higher the NMI value is, the more similar between two clusters. This similarity measure can only be applied when the real solution of the problem is known.

4.3. Summary

An algorithm cannot be justified as correct without testing it. Real-world networks and synthetic networks are essential for testing a community detection algorithm. Once an algorithm is tested using dataset, the next step is to assess the quality of the outputs produced by the algorithm. In order to find good communities a proper quality function that should be intuitive and easy to agree upon is necessary. A review of frequently used quality measures both for disjoint and overlapping communities are discussed in this chapter.

The necessity and importance of real-world networks and synthetic networks has been discussed. The real-world networks that are used to test the developed algorithm have been listed. The common benchmarks used in the community detection research and its importance has been explained. To evaluate the goodness of a community, if it is represented through a quantitative value, then it will be more meaningful. A quality measure that is suitable for disjoint community detection may not be suitable for overlapping community detection. Hence, a variety of measures have been proposed by various researchers both for real-world networks and artificial networks. A detailed description about various quality metrics used for evaluating the communities detected by the algorithms are listed.

CHAPTER V

LABEL PROPAGATION ALGORITHMS

There exist various algorithms that identify community structures in large-scale real-world networks which requires prior information about the number and size of communities. The size of the community is often not predictable beforehand in many complex networks, particularly in social networks. In online social networks where the network size is huge and heterogeneous, it is not possible to guess the number of communities at first and it is computationally expensive to determine the community size. Label Propagation algorithm detect community structures using network structure alone as its guide and requires no prior information about communities. This chapter presents an overview of label propagation algorithms.

5.1. Introduction

In multi-state spin models (Reichardt and Bornholdt 2004) a spin is assigned to each node. This model can be applied to community detection. Potts model is one among the most popular models in statistical mechanics. Q-state Potts model is one such model (Reichardt and Bornholdt 2008), where q is the number of states that a spin may take, indicating the maximum number of communities. Label Propagation Algorithm (LPA) is shown to be equivalent to a Potts model (Tibely and Kertz 2008). It belongs to the family of agent-based community detection algorithms.

The idea of label flooding through a network originated from the L-shell method proposed by Bagrow (2005). The intuition of LPA flooding is that a single label can quickly become dominant in a densely connected group of vertices whereas it has trouble crossing a sparsely connected region, or in a sense it is trapped inside a densely connected group of vertices. The author proposed a local community detection method where a node is initialized with a label and propagates step by step via neighbors until the end of the community. The end of the community indicates the number of edges proceeding outward from the community and drops below a threshold value.

Label spreading can be considered as a simplified but specific case of epidemic spreading of diseases where individuals are considered with infectious with their own unique disease. In the case of epidemic spreading, each person is infected by a disease that is spreading or existing in their neighborhood. Similar to the process of disease spreading in epidemic network, label spreading can be treated in computer networks as community formation problem. As the spreading progresses the number of labels decreases gradually at each iteration and some labels may vanish due to domination of other labels. At the end of iteration, certain labels exist and dominate the whole network forming communities. But, due to the epidemic nature of the algorithm, certain labels form giant communities, which is the major limitation of label propagation algorithms.

LPA can also be considered as a simple opinion spreading model but with many competing opinions. During the opinion spreading process, each node adopts a opinion through an artificial unique identifier in agreement with the majority of its neighbors. At the end of the opinion spreading process, connected nodes with the same id form a community. In social network, a user can view, spread, accept or reject an opinion received from its neighbors. Labels of each node can be treated as opinion in the LPA. Propagating the labels is similar to opinion spreading in social network. Opinions are chosen based on the opinions of the neighbor list, which in turn, form their opinions from their neighbors and so on. This resembles the characteristics of social network where a user adds the friend's friend into their friends list.

LPA algorithm provides desirable qualities such as easy implementation, fast execution and it is more suitable for the analysis of large systems. Due to their fast execution, label propagation techniques are considered as more suitable for the analysis of large systems. In this Chapter various label propagation algorithms that are capable to detect disjoint and overlapping communities are discussed.

5.2. Label Propagation

LPA which was first proposed by Raghavan et al. (2007) uses unique identifiers of nodes as labels and propagated the labels based on an agreement with the majority of the neighbor nodes. Each node selects a label from its neighborhood to adopt it as its label. The main idea behind Label Propagation Algorithm is to propagate the labels of node throughout the network using some techniques and form communities through this label propagation itself. The Label Propagation Algorithm (LPA) is a method which is effective, simple and near-linear time algorithm.

Label Propagation Algorithms work as follows: Node x has neighbors $X_1, X_2 X_3, \ldots X_n$ and each neighbor carries a label denoting the community to which they belong to. Each node in the network chooses to join the community to which the maximum number of its neighbors belongs to, with ties broken uniformly and randomly. At the beginning, every node is initialized with unique label (called as identifier) and the labels propagate through the network. At every step of propagation, each node updates its label based on the labels of its neighbors. As labels propagate, densely connected groups of nodes quickly reach a consensus on a unique label as shown in Figure. 5.1.

At end of the propagation, most labels will disappear and some label may dominate. Label propagation algorithm reaches convergence when each vertex has the majority label of its neighbors. At the end of the convergence, nodes connected with the same label form a community. According to LPA, communities are defined as vertices having identical labels at convergence. The agreement between the nodes to spread the labels forms the basis for Label propagation algorithms.

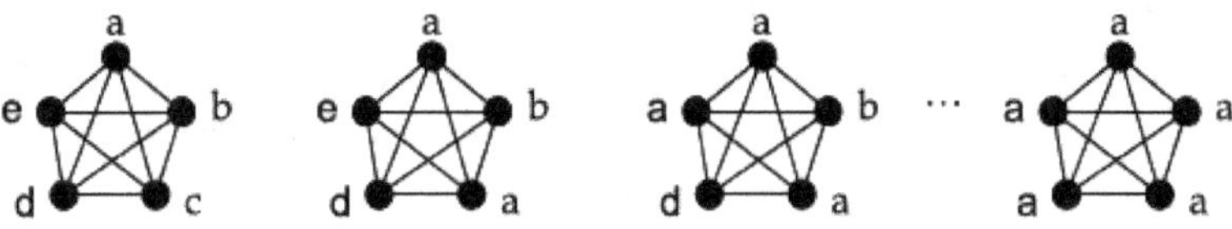

Figure 5.1: Node Labels are Updated from Left to Right (Raghavan et al. 2007)

The label updation can be done either synchronously or asynchronously. In the process of label propagation, at an instance there will be some nodes in the network that have undergone an iteration and some others may not have undergone an iteration.

1. In synchronous updating, a node x at t^{th} iteration updates its label based on the labels of its neighbors at iteration $t-1$.

   Hence, $C_x(t) = f\left(C_{x1}(t-1), C_{x2}(t-1), \ldots C_{xk}(t-1)\right)$ where $C_x(t)$ is the label of node x at time t.

2. In asynchronous updating, a node at t^{th} iteration, updates its label based on the labels of its neighbors at iteration t as well as $t-1$. The new labels of the nodes which have undergone the updating during the current iteration t is taken, and for the nodes which have not undergone the updation during the current iteration t, the labels at $(t-1)^{th}$ iteration is taken. Hence, $C_x(t) = f\left(C_{x_i1}(t), \ldots, C_{x_im}(t), C_{x_i(m+1)}(t-1), \ldots, C_{x_ik}(t-1)\right)$,

   where $x_{i1} \ldots x_{im}$ are neighbors of x that have already been updated in the current iteration while $x_{i(m+1)} \ldots x_{ik}$ are neighbors that are not yet updated in the current iteration.

The order of nodes to be updated at each iteration is randomly chosen. At the beginning of the algorithm, there are n different labels and as iteration progresses the number of labels reduces. The iteration should be performed until no node in the network changes its labels or until a stop condition is satisfied. At the end of the iteration, there are as many labels as there are communities. LPA algorithm is shown in Figure 5.2.

LPA belongs to the family of agent based community detection algorithms. Due to the random tie breaking strategy, the algorithm produced different solutions at different runs. The stop criterion of this algorithm is similar to the definition of strong communities proposed by Radicchi et al (2004). Each node in strong communities are expected to have strictly more neighbors within its community than outside, the communities obtained by the label propagation process require each node to have at least as many neighbors within its community as it has with each of the other communities.

The authors pointed out that even though they obtained different community structures at different runs, they were similar to each other. It is difficult to pick one solution as the best one among several different results, because one solution may be able to identify a community that was not discovered in the other and vice-versa. Hence, an aggregate of all the different solutions were found that provides a community structure containing the most useful information.

Since LPA algorithms are considered as fast and efficient, much research work has been progressed in the last decade. A major advantage of this algorithm in comparison with most other graph clustering algorithms is that it totally relies only on local information that can be quickly computed. Each node makes its own decision regarding the community to which it belongs to based on the communities of its immediate neighbors. Raghavan et al. (2007) found that irrespective of the number of nodes, 95% of the nodes are classified correctly by the end of the 5th iteration. When the algorithm terminates it is possible that two or more disconnected groups of nodes have the same label because two or more neighbors of a node received its label and pass the labels in different directions, which ultimately leads to different communities adapting the same label. To separate this disconnected components, a simple breath-first search on the sub-networks was run after the termination of algorithm.

Step 1	Initialize the labels at all nodes in the network. For a given node x, $C_x(0) = x$
Step 2	Set $t = 1$.
Step 3	Arrange the nodes in the network in a random order and set it to X.
Step 4	For each $x \in X$ chosen in a specific order, let $$C_x(t) = f\left(C_{x_i1}(t), \ldots, C_{x_im}(t), C_{x_i(m+1)}(t-1), \ldots, C_{x_ik}(t-1)\right)$$ f here returns the label occurring with the highest frequency among neighbors and ties are broken uniformly randomly.
Step 5	If every node has a label that the maximum number of their neighbors has, then stop the algorithm, else, set $t = t + 1$ and go to step 3.

Figure 5.2: Steps Involved in Label Propagation Algorithm

The authors pointed that if the set of nodes in the network that are likely to act as centers of attraction for their respective communities are known, then it would be sufficient to initialize such nodes with unique labels, leaving the remaining nodes unlabeled. If this algorithm is applied after identifying center nodes, then, the unlabeled nodes will have a tendency to acquire labels from their closest attractor and join that community. Also, restricting the set of nodes initialized with labels will reduce the range of possible solutions that the algorithm can produce. Since identifying such center nodes are difficult before identifying the community itself, in this algorithm all nodes are given equal importance and provided with unique labels before iteration starts.

The main advantage of LPA is its near linear-time complexity. It runs linearly in the number of edges, thus linearly also in the number of nodes for sparse network. The number of iterations to converge appears independent of graph size, or growing very slowly with it. Initializing every node with unique labels require $O(n)$ time. Each iteration takes linear time in the number of edges $O(m)$ and the time for processing disconnected communities is $O(m+n)$. As the number of iteration increases, the number of nodes that are classified correctly increases. This algorithm formed the basis for all the succeeding label propagation algorithms.

Numerous algorithms have been developed using Label Propagation techniques to detect disjoint communities (Raghavan et al. 2007; Leung et al.. 2009; Subelj and Bajac 2011; Xie et al. 2013) as well as for overlapping communities(Gregory 2010; Xie et al. 2011; Wu et al. 2012). Many of these algorithms attempt to detect either disjoint or overlapping communities from static networks. There are few algorithms that detect communities from dynamic networks also (Cazabet et al. 2010). Algorithms that use labels for communication between networks to form communities in static network are discussed in the Section 5.3

5.3. LPA for Disjoint Community Detection

In LPA proposed by Raghavan et al. (2007), a label can spread too far from its origin and produce a single large community (monster communities) when applied to large web networks. Monster communities occupy more than half the nodes of the network. Leung (Leung et al. 2009) focused mainly on the problem of monster communities on large web networks and significantly improved the performance of community detection using label hop attenuation technique. This technique prevents the label from spreading too from its origin. Each label l_n is associated with additional score s_n that is initially set to the value of 1 and decreases after each propagation as shown below.

$$s_n = (\max_{i \in N^{cn}(n)} s_i) - \delta$$

(where δ being the attenuation ratio).

When s_n reaches 0, the label stops propagating, thus eliminating the formation of a single large community. With hop attenuation the authors coupled node preference f_n which represents the node propagation strength, to achieve better performance of the LPA. The label propagating updation rule is modified as

$$c_n = \arg \max_{l} \sum_{i \in N^l(n)} f_i^{\alpha} s_i w_{ni}$$

where w_{ni} is the edge weight (equal to 1 for unweighted graphs) and ɑ is a parameter of the algorithm. Hop attenuation has proven to be a reliable technique for preventing monster communities. It has also been observed that hop attention may damage some reasonable large communities since it limits the radius of community structure. Predicting the value of attenuation ration δ has been the main issue of this algorithm. Leung et al. (2009) used the values around 0.10 for δ and obtained good results. The authors have also observed that large values of δ may prevent the natural growth of communities and have proposed a dynamic strategy that decreases δ from 0:50 towards 0. In the early iterations of the algorithm, large values of δ prevent a single label propagating too far to form strong communities. The value of δ is then decreased, to gradually relax the restriction and to allow formation of the actual communities that exists in the network topology. From the experiments on real-world networks, the authors proved that such a strategy has very good performance on larger networks.

Subelj and Bajec (2011) advanced the algorithm developed by Leung et al. (2009) and proposed different dynamic hop attenuation strategies, based on the hypothesis that hop attenuation should only be employed, when a community, or a set of communities, is rapidly occupying a large portion of the network. Otherwise the labels should be allowed to reach the equilibrium unrestrained. This approach would retain the dynamics of label propagation and still prevent the emergence of a major community.

The authors considered several strategies for detecting the emergence of a large community or a set of large communities and developed two unique strategies of community formation namely defensive preservation of communities, where preference is given to the nodes in the core of each community, and offensive expansion of communities, where preference is given to the border nodes of each community. They proposed an advanced label propagation algorithm: the diffusion and propagation algorithm (DPA) that combines the two strategies in a hierarchical manner. The algorithm first applies the defensive strategy to the original network to produce large number of smaller communities (i.e. initial estimates of the communities). It then applies propagation strength to the core of each community, i.e.

$f_n^{\alpha} = p_n$. Thus the updating rule

$$c_n = \arg \max_{l} \sum_{i \in N^l(n)} f_i^{\alpha} s_i w_{ni}$$

proposed by Leung et al. (2009) is modified as

$$c_n = \arg \max_{l} \sum_{i \in N^l(n))} p_i s_i w_{ni}$$

The labels of all the border nodes of a community are relabeled such that approximately one half of the nodes retain their original label. Then, the offensive strategy is applied on the constructed community network to extract the core of the network and resulted in whisker communities. The offensive strategy applies preference to the border of each community, i.e.,

$f_n^{\alpha} = 1 - p_n$ and the updating rule is modified as

$$c_n = \arg \max_{l} \sum_{i \in N'(n)} (1 - p_i)s_i w_{ni}$$

The above two strategies are recursively applied only to the core of the community, when the whisker communities are retained as unidentified communities. The recursion process is repeated until the extracted core contains all of the nodes of the network analyzed. From the experiments, the authors suggested that dynamic hop attenuation strategy should only be employed, when a community, or a set of communities, is rapidly occupying a large portion of the network. If it does not occupy a large portion of the network, the restriction should be relaxed allowing the label propagation to reach the equilibrium unrestrained. This approach would retain the dynamics of label propagation as well as prevent the emergence of a monster community. DPA employs only local measures for community detection, and does not require the number of communities to be specified beforehand. At each iteration of the algorithm, each edge of the network is visited (at most) twice. Thus the time complexity of a single iteration equals $O(m)$, with m being the number of edges.

In Label propagation algorithm proposed by Raghavan et al. (2007), at the early stage of the propagation process, the fraction of attempted updates that result in changes to new labels is high because most nodes are in a very diverse neighborhood. But, after few iterations, the competition between communities is restricted only to their boundaries. Updates are unnecessary for nodes inside the community (passive nodes) as they do not change their labels after few iteration. The unnecessary updates of labels that fail to change their labels require additional time. So, the final convergence of LPA is delayed. This time delay can be easily reduced by book keeping the information about the boundaries of the currently existing communities.

In order to improve the execution time of LPA, Xie and Szymanski (2011) proposed an update rule based on neighborhood strength driven label propagation. The basic idea of the improvement is to avoid unnecessary updates in each iteration of the algorithm, while maintaining the overall behavior of the algorithm and achieve higher speed of execution to improve the quality of the community detection. By storing the information about the community boundaries, this algorithm saved the amount of time by avoiding re-calculation. This improvement does not require any threshold value or modification of the stop criterion.

The authors referred nodes whose neighbors have the same label as interior nodes and nodes that are not interior as boundary nodes. Nodes that attempt to change their labels during updation were called as active and nodes that do not change their labels were said as passive nodes. A node can be in three states: passive interior, passive boundary, active boundary. A boundary node could be either passive or active depending on its neighborhood. The updating rule itself becomes a natural end of execution condition. The algorithm stops when every node becomes passive (i.e. convergence of a network) and detects only disjoint communities. The algorithm is shown in Figure 5.3.

1. At time t=0, construct the active node list containing all the nodes.
2. Randomly pick an active node, say i, from the list and attempt to adopt a new label according to the update rule. Since only active nodes are placed initially on the list and they remain on the list as long as they are active, each node selected for an update will change its label during the update.
3. First, check if the updated node became passive and if so, remove it from the list. Next, check all its neighbors for the change of status in the following three steps.
    a. If an interior neighbor became an active boundary node, add it to the active node list.
    b. Remove any previously active neighbor that became passive from the active node list.
    c. Add any previously passive boundary neighbor that became active to the active node list.
    d. If the active node list is empty, stop; otherwise, increase time t by one unit and go to step 2.

Figure 5.3: Neighborhood Strength Driven Label Propagation (Xie et al. 2011)

The complexity of the improved algorithm is unchanged. Initialization of the active node list requires $O(n)$ time. For randomly selecting a node $O(1)$ time is required. Updating the node i and its neighbors requires $O(d_i)$, where d_i is the degree of node i. By using the active node list, evaluating the convergence of the whole network is easy and takes exactly

$O(1)$ by checking if the list is empty. The author proved that the number of iterations needed for the algorithm to converge is equal to the total number of effective updates.

Xie J. and Szymanski B. K. (2013) proposed a stabilized Label Propagation Algorithm by introducing a set of operators to control and stabilize the propagation dynamics. They stabilized LPA and extended Markov Cluster Algorithm (MCL) approach that resulted in LabelRank algorithm. It stores, propagates and ranks labels in each node and relies on four operators namely propagation, inflation, cutoff and conditional update to stabilize the propagation dynamics. In this algorithm, an entire distribution of labels is maintained using n $1 \times n$ vectors (n is the number of nodes in the network) that is different from adjacency matrix defining the network structure. Each element of the probability matrix holds the current estimation of probability of node i observing label $c \in C$ taken from a finite set C. Initially, the probability matrix of the network is represented as

$$P_i(c) = \frac{1}{k_i} \ \forall \, c \ s.t. A_{ic} = 1$$

During the propagation process each node broadcasts the nodes to its neighbors at each time step and computes the new distribution $P_i(c)$ simultaneously as

$$P_j^{'}(c) = \sum_{j \in Nb(i)} P_j(c) / k_i, \forall c \in C$$

where $Nb(.)$ is a set of neighbors of node i and $k_i = | Nb(.) |$ is the number of neighbors. In matrix form this operator can be expressed as $A * P$, where A is the $n \times n$ adjacency matrix and P is the $n \times n$ label distribution matrix. Since each node keeps multiple labels received from its neighbors, LabelRank eliminates the need of tie breaking problem as in LPA and COPRA. A community is formed of nodes with same highest probability.

In the second step of LabelRank, inflation operator Γ_{in} is used on P to contract the propagation, where   is the parameter taking real values. In MCL, the inflation is applied to adjacency matrix. But, in LabelRank, the inflation operator was applied to the label distribution matrix P (instead of a stochastic matrix or adjacency matrix) to decouple it from the network structure. After applying inflation operator

$$\Gamma_{in}P(c) = P_i(c)^{in} / \sum_{j \in C} P_i(j)^{in}$$

Each value in $P_i(c)$ changes to $P_i(c)^{in}$. This operator increases the probabilities of labels that were assigned high probability during propagation and decrease the probabilities of labels that were assigned low probability during propagation. To reduce the memory utilization, an cutoff operator is applied to P to remove labels that are below threshold value. Inflation helps to decrease probabilities of labels to which propagation assigned low probability and cutoff efficiently reduces the space complexity, from quadratic to linear. Due to cutoff and inflation operators, the number of labels in each node monotonically decreases and drops to a small constant within few steps. Since, LabelRank detects the highest quality communities far before convergence and if the iteration continues after convergence, the quality of the detected communities decreases. Inspite of the above three operations there is no guarantee for good performance of algorithm. Hence a novel solution based on the conditional update operator is used to update a node only when it is significantly different from its neighbors in terms of labels. Conditional update preserves detected communities and detects termination based on scarcity of changes to the network. At each iteration, the change is accepted only by nodes that satisfy the following update condition

$$\sum_{j \in Nb(i)} isSubset\left(C_i^*, C_j^*\right) \leq q\kappa_i$$

Introduction of the new operator, conditional rule and stopping criteria preserves the speed of the LPA based algorithms. The output is deterministic because there is no randomness in the simulation. The operators resolve the randomness issue that is present in traditional LPA, by stabilizing the discovered communities in all runs of the same network. The LabelRank algorithm is shown in Figure 5.4. The running time of LabelRank is $O(m)$, linear with the number of edges m. Adding selfloop takes $O(n)$, initialization of P takes $O(m)$, each of the four operators takes $O(m)$ on average and the number of iterations is usually $O(1)$. The author suggested that such type of stabilization as used in this algorithm is important for the class of all label propagation algorithms. Because, without stabilization, these type of algorithms cannot be applied to dynamic networks.

$$
\boxed{
\begin{array}{l}
\text{add selfloop to adjacency matrix } A \\[6pt]
\text{initialize label distribution } P \\[6pt]
\text{repeat} \\[6pt]
\quad P^{'} = A \times P \\[6pt]
\quad P^{'} = \Gamma_{in} P^{'} \\[6pt]
\quad P^{'} = \Phi_{r} P^{'} \\[6pt]
\quad P = \Theta_{q}(P^{'}, P) \\[6pt]
\text{until stop criterion satisfied} \\[6pt]
\text{output communities based on } P
\end{array}
}
$$

Figure 5.4: Overall Procedure of LabelRank Algorithm (Xie et al. 2013)

5.4. Overlapping Community Detection

COPRA is the first algorithm proposed to detect overlapping community using label propagation which is very fast and allows each vertex to belong to multiple communities at a time (Gregory 2010). In Label Propagation algorithm designed by Raghavan et al. (2007), a vertex contains single label to which it belongs. To find overlapping communities a vertex should contain more than one label. In COPRA, each vertex x is labeled with a set of pairs (c, b), where c is a community identifier and b is the belonging coefficient that indicates the strength of x's membership of community c such that all belonging coefficient for x sum to 1. During the label propagation process, label of x is set to the union of its neighbors label, belonging coefficients of the communities over all neighbors is summed and normalized.

The label of a vertex in iteration t is always based on its neighbors label in iteration $t-1$. To retain more than one community identifier in each label, the algorithm deletes the pairs whose belonging coefficient is less than some threshold value $(1/v)$, where v is the parameter of the algorithm. If all pairs in a vertex label have a belonging coefficient less than the threshold, a pair that has the greatest belonging coefficient is retained and all others are deleted. If more than one pair has the same belonging coefficient below the threshold, then a random pair is selected. The output of the algorithm is non-deterministic due to its random selection.

Gregory (2010) suggested that using synchronous updating, results proved to be better than asynchronous updating as done by LPA and Leung et al. (2009). In order to prevent community identifier propagating too far and forming monster communities, after a propagating step, a vertex is checked whether it is still among the community identifier labeling vertex x. If so, the label of x is set to x only and all other community identifiers are deleted. This technique proved to improve the worst results because label x appears on x more than once and reduces the size of other communities because other communities no longer include x. Though, this technique was successful in improving the worst result, best results were also worsened due to the limits imposed on community size. At the end of the propagation, each vertex whose labels contains community identifier c is placed in community c. This method might form communities that are subset of others. COPRA avoided this by keeping track of the subset relationships between communities and deleting a community, i.e., a subset of other.

Similar to LPA, the communities may not be connected at the end in COPRA also. So, all disconnected communities are split into smaller connected ones. A novel termination condition is used to terminate the algorithm with the good solution. For low overlapping density networks, COPRA offers better performance. But, it produces a number of small size communities in some networks due to the global vertex-independent parameter. Even though the algorithm produces different solutions each time it is run, all the solutions are good ones. If the values of the parameter v is greater, the algorithm deletes greater overlaps between communities. If the value of the v increases too much, community identifier starts propagating too far and the algorithm produces worst results. The execution time is lightly more than the linear time followed by LPA, but faster than CFinder and CONGO. According to the comparative analysis of various algorithms on benchmarks of Lancichinetti A. and Fortunato S. (2009), COPRA has been marked as the most effective method once fed with correct parameters. The main procedure of COPRA is given in Figure 5.5.

1. To initialize, every vertex is given a unique label with belonging coefficient setting to 1.

2. Then, repeatedly, each vertex *x* updates its labels by summing and normalizing the belonging coefficients of vertices in the neighbor set of *x* To avoid every vertex owning all community identifiers at the end, COPRA algorithm uses the parameter *v* to limit the maximum number of communities to which any vertex can belong. Propagation stops if stop criterion is satisfied.

3. Remove communities that are totally contained by others.

4. Split discontinuous communities.

Figure 5.5: Overall procedure of COPRA (Gregory 2010)

If n is the number of vertices and m is the number of edges and v is the parameter (maximum number of communities per vertex), then the time complexity of COPRA in each phase is

1. Initialization takes time $O(n)$

2. For constructing an updated label for each of the n vertices is $O(vm \log(vm / n))$

3. For iterating through all community identifiers of each of the n vertices the total time is $O(vn)$. For repeated iteration, time per iteration is $O(v(m + n) + v^3 n))$ and the initial and final steps take time $O(v(m + n) + v^3 n))$.

Xie (Xie et al. 2011) proposed a fast Speaker-listener Label Propagation Algorithm (SLPA), which spreads labels according to dynamic interaction rules and maintains label distributions in the memory of each node. In SLPA, each node can be a speaker or a listener depending on whether it serves as an information provider or consumer. A node stores as many labels as it likes, based on the propagation experience in the stochastic processes which is driven by the underlying network structure. The more a node observes a label the more likely it will spread this label to other nodes. This is similar to mimicking people's preference of spreading most discussed opinions. The algorithm is shown in Figure 5.6.

The significant characteristics of SLPA are:

a. a node accumulates knowledge of repeatedly observed labels instead of erasing all but one of them

b. no knowledge about the number of communities is required.

SLPA follows asynchronous updating scheme for updating the labels in the memory. The noteworthy feature of SLPA is memory for each node takes into account information that has been observed in the *past* to make current decision. This feature is not followed in other label propagation algorithms like LPA and CORPA, where a node updates its label completely forgetting the old knowledge. This feature combines the accuracy of the asynchronous update with the stability of the synchronous update due to which the fragmentation issues (producing a number of small size communities) that is present in COPRA is avoided in SLPA. The algorithm simply stops when the predefined maximum number of iterations T is reached. In general, SLPA produces relatively stable outputs, independent of network size or structure, when T is greater than 20.

The algorithm which is shown in Figure 5.6 efficiently identifies both node and community level overlapping structures. It is suitable for weighted, un-weighted, directed and undirected networks, but due to random tie breaking strategy, it produces different partitions in different runs, which is not desirable in applications like tracking the evolution of communities in a dynamic network. The initialization of labels requires $O(n)$ time, where n is the total number of nodes. The outer loop is controlled by the user defined maximum iteration T. The inner loop is controlled by n. One speaking rule and one listening rule is followed in inner loop. For the speaking rule, selecting an element from the array requires $O(1)$ operation. For listening rule, since the listener needs to check all the labels from its neighbors, it takes $O(k)$ on average, where k is the average degree. The complexity of the dynamic evolution for the asynchronous update is $O(Tm)$ and $O(Tn)$ on an arbitrary network and sparse network respectively. Since each node has a memory of size T, in the post-processing, the thresholding operation requires $O(Tn)$ operations. The time complexity of the entire algorithm is $O(Tn)$ in sparse networks.

Algorithm : SLPA(T, r)
1) First, the memory of each node is initialized with this node's id (i.e., with a unique label). 2) Then, the following steps are repeated until the stop criterion is satisfied: a. One unvisited node is randomly selected as a listener. b.Each neighbor of the selected node sends out a *single* label following certain *speaking rule*, such as selecting a random label from its memory with probability proportional to the occurrence frequency of this label in the memory. c. The listener accepts *one* label from the collection of labels received from neighbors following certain *listening rule*, such as selecting the most popular label from what it observed in the *current* step. The listener adds the most popular label received to its memory. d. Mark the listener visited. 3) Finally, the post-processing based on the labels in the memories and the threshold r is applied to output the communities.

Figure 5.6: SLPA Algorithm (Xie et al. 2011)

In COPRA, as v is vertex independent, if there are some vertices with a small number of community memberships and some others with a large number of community memberships, it will be hard for COPRA to choose a suitable v to satisfy both kinds of vertices at the same time. To solve this problem Wu et al. (2012) proposed a new balanced multi-label propagation algorithm (BMLPA) using a balanced belonging coefficients update strategy with vertex dependent parameter to detect overlapping communities in networks with various numbers of community memberships, which cannot be solved well by COPRA algorithm. In the COPRA algorithm, each vertex has at most v labels, while the balanced belonging coefficients (BBC) update strategy proposed by the author does not limit the number of communities that a vertex v may belong to. The update strategy of the algorithm requires that labels of a vertex have balanced belonging coefficients and it allows vertices to belong to any number of communities without a global limit on the largest number of community memberships as in COPRA.

A rough core (RC) extraction method is designed in BMLPA to initialize labels before label propagation. As many maximal cliques that highly overlap only indicate the same core, the problem is for a core indicated by more than one clique, i.e., which clique should be extracted to initialize the labels. Since monster communities can be formed from larger cliques, the author suggested that smaller cliques will be better for the final results. The rough core indicates the smallest maximal clique starting from two first chosen vertices. The author proved that RC initialization and the BBC update strategy can bring improvements in both quality and stability, especially for networks that contain vertices with various numbers of community memberships. In n is the number of nodes and m is the number of edges, v_{avg} is the average number of labels to which each vertex belong and d_{avg} is the average degree, then the time complexity of BMLPA is :for initialization $O(n(\log n + v_{avg} d_{avg}))$, for propagation $O(v_{avg} m \log(v_{avg} m / n))$ with total time complexity of $O(n \log n)$ per iteration.

Li et al. (2012) improved the LPA algorithm by using a node score which uncovers hub preference to detect overlapping community structure in complex network. In this algorithm, community sizes were considered into weights of edges avoiding monster communities. Raghavan et al. (2007) claimed that LPA could identify hub nodes as those which kept oscillating among several communities. However this identification process will lead to huge computational cost and unable to uncover the hub's preference. To solve this issue, the author observed the hub nodes among communities and found that hub nodes connect different communities with approximate weight and proposed a measurement D_x to present the hub preference of node i as follows:

$$Dx\left(i\right) = \frac{\sum_{k \in l_i} \left(W_i(k) - \overline{W_i}\right)^2}{n}$$

where

$$\overline{W_i} = \frac{\sum_{k \in l_i} W_i(k)}{n}$$

is the average of $W_i(k)$ and n is the number of elements in l_i . The smaller $Dx\left(i\right)$ is, the more probable that node i is hub node. When, $Dx\left(i\right) = 0$ it means node i equally connects with all the communities. The value of threshold δ uncover the scope of overlapping in complex network. The author modified LPA using $Dx\left(i\right)$ and δ to detect overlapping communities. During each propagation step, only nodes whose measurement Dx larger than δ can be infected by their neighbors.

In asynchronous implementation of the LPA algorithm, each node calculates Dx in propagation step, so the modification does not increase computing time complexity. If *N is* the number of nodes in complex network and *K* is number of iteration, the computational cost of the improved algorithm is $O(KN)$ which is also near linear time. In this algorithm, the nodes were sorted according to smaller values of Dx in each update step in order to further improve computational cost of the proposed algorithm. Moreover, the community size was taken into consideration for the process of generating node label to prevent monster community structure. The label is updated based on the following criterion

$$L_i^{'} = \arg\max_{K} \frac{W_i(k)}{|K|^{\frac{1}{2}}} K \in l_i$$

which can prevent monster community structure. Figure 5.7 lists the steps involved in the above mentioned algorithm.

1	Initialize each node in complex network with a unique label and then calculate the measurement Dx . Sort all the nodes according to the value of Dx x in descending order and then put the sorted nodes into queue Q.
2	For each node v in Q, update its label. when $Dx(v) \geq \delta$. The parameter δ which decides the scope of overlapping is preliminary set. Resort all nodes according to Dx and put them into Q.
3	When none node updates its label or the iteration time is greater than a given threshold stop the algorithm. Otherwise, go to step 2.

Figure 5.7: A Label Propagation Algorithm Using Hub Preference

Wu et al. (2013) proposed a novel weighted label propagation algorithm (WLPA), as an extension of SLPA, by introducing a similarity between any two vertices in a network based on the labels each vertex has received during label propagation and using this similarity as a weight of the edge between the two vertices in the next iteration of label propagation. Further, weights were added to an edge of two vertices that could be repeated in multiple label propagations, making it possible to refine the communities found in each repetition.

SLPA outperforms the original LPA with extra information that is the array of labels. To improve SLPA, the author introduced weight similarities as an extra information to SLPA. The similarity of any vertices in a network is calculated as a weight of edge between the two vertices and this is passed to SLPA. The overview of WLPA algorithm is shown in Figure 5.8.

Step 1.	Run SPLA with steps 1 and 2 above.
Step 2.	Use the last 20% of the labels each vertex has received to compute the similarity between any two vertices.
Step 3.	Run SPLA using this similarity as a weight of the edge between the two vertices.

Figure 5.8: Weighted Label Propagation Algorithm (WLPA)

5.5. Summary

Label propagation techniques are the simplest techniques for identifying communities in complex networks. It is considered as one of the fastest algorithm due to its near linear time complexity. This chapter summarized an overview of various algorithms that detects overlapping communities in static network using the label propagation techniques.

CHAPTER VI

MULTI-LABEL PROPAGATION

Depending on the structure of the network, community detection algorithms can be classified as disjoint and overlapping. Numerous algorithms have been proposed for detecting both disjoint and overlapping communities on static networks and dynamic network. A detailed list of most popular disjoint and overlapping community detection algorithms designed for static networks are listed in this chapter.

6.1. Multi-Label Propagation[MLPA]

Label Propagation algorithms that use single labels for propagation face the problem of random tie breaking when choosing a label among a set of labels for propagation. Due to the random tie breaking nature, techniques that follow single label for propagation produces non-deterministic outputs. Designing a multi-label propagation algorithm to detect overlapping communities involves propagation of more than one label during the community detection process. The major objective of any multi-label propagation algorithms is to formulate a decision for choosing multiple labels for propagation and storing multiple labels received from the propagation process. This chapter presents a multi-label propagation approach which has three important phases:

- Sending labels other nodes
- Listening labels from other nodes for deciding which label to choose from the set of labels received from other nodes
- Updating the nodes.

All the three phases relies on the propagation process in the network. Hence, first the propagation functionalities should be proposed to ensure that multiple labels are propagated between nodes in the network. Therefore, as a first step of the design, label propagation constraints are formulated. The nodes are categorized as speaker nodes and listener nodes and the constraints are imposed on the two categories. The algorithm treats each node in the network as both speaker and listener. When a specific node starts gathering the labels from the adjacent nodes, it acts as an information consumer. Whereas, when it sends labels to the adjacent nodes it acts as an information provider. Until the listener asks for the labels from speaker, no labels are propagated from node to node. In this research work, each node broad casts multiple labels to the neighbour nodes and at the same time receives multiple labels from its neighbours.

To start with, each node is assigned a unique label. During the iteration, every speaker sends multiple labels to the listener based on certain rules. Listener accepts a label or set of labels send by the speaker based on specified rules. Different algorithms use different strategies to propagate and update a label. In SLPA, at each iteration, a label that has a maximum probability is send by the speaker. The listener listens to all the labels send by the neighbour nodes, but, accepts only one label that has maximum number of occurrence. MLPA aims to modify this particular process of speaking rule and listening rule by using multiple labels for speaking and listening. The approach of passing multiple labels between speaker and listener is the main difference between SLPA and MLPA. This system has been designed as a collection of agents that determine the following process:

- Which labels should be sent to the neighbour nodes during the propagation?
- Which labels are to be accepted from the received labels?
- How to assign probabilities?
- How to update the labels and stabilize it?
- When to stop the propagation?

The critical issue related to the first three questions is how information should be maintained and it solely relies on the criteria formulated in the system. Depending upon the criterion chosen by the agents, labels propagate to form communities. This chapter discusses about agents designed for the system and elaborates the criteria used for identifying overlapping communities in social network. An important problem in label propagation algorithms are its randomness in the output. Due to the random tie breaking strategies followed in various label propagation algorithms, every time when an algorithm is executed different outputs are produced. Though the number of communities may be approximately same in all the runs, the label of communities might change due to the dynamics in the criteria used by the algorithms. The objective of this research work is to design an algorithm that detects community overlap by avoiding the random tie breaking strategy followed in SLPA and produce deterministic communities. This work provides further understanding on dynamics of label propagation, in particular, how different propagation strategies can alter the dynamics of the process.

6.2.   Basic Notations

An undirected, unweighted graph $G = (V, E)$ consisting of a vertex (node) set V and edge set E is represented as a social network. Let n and m be the number of nodes and edges in the network. V is the set of n nodes and E is the set of m connections. The notation $(u, v) \in E$ represents there is a link between two nodes u and v. The graph is represented mathematically by an adjacency matrix A. In terms of social network with n individuals, the social relationships between different individual is represented by the adjacency matrix. The degree of a node i is defined as the number of adjacent nodes of i. For a node $i \in V$, let $|K_i|$ denote its degree.

A partition $P = \{P_1, P_2, P_3, \ldots P_n\}$ is a division of network into disjoint communities, where P denotes the partition composed of n non-overlapping communities. In a pair of communities P_i and P_j, if $P_i \cap P_j = 0 \; \forall i \neq j$ then it is said as disjoint communities. A cover or network community structure is represented as $C = \{C_1, C_2, C_3, \ldots, C_n\}$ i.e. a collection of subset of V where each $C_i \in C$ and its subgraph form a community of G. If node belongs to more than one community such as C_i and C_j, then there exists a pair of community C_i and C_j such that $C_i \cap C_j \neq 0 \; \forall \; i \neq j$.

Given an undirected, unweighted network $N(n, m)$, where is n the number of nodes and m is the number of connections in the network, the objective of this work is to detect communities, $C_1, C_2, C_3, \ldots C_P$, where a node in the network N belongs to more than one community. Initially, before the algorithm starts, the network N is assumed to contain n communities represented as $C = \{C_1, C_2, C_3, \ldots C_n\}$. The objective of the label propagation algorithm is to reduce the number of communities to p such that $p<n$ and form communities $C_1, C_2, C_3, \ldots, C_p$. The number of communities to be detected is not known or neither received as a parameter form the user which is the main characteristic of all label propagation algorithms.

Complex networks are normally huge in size and explicit information of their size and subgroups are not known in advance. Given a complex network, the objective of a community detection problem is to find whether inherent similarity or an externally specified similarity among the nodes of the network exists or not. Hence, the goal of a community detection algorithm is to identify the number of communities in spite of lack of knowledge about the size of network. Based on the above assumption, MLPA, uses multiple labels for propagation as well as for updation to detect community overlaps in the network using only the network structure as its guide. An algorithm with near-linear time complexity and which produces deterministic communities that avoids the dynamics in communities is essential to detect overlapping communities.

The problem is based on the idea of label flooding algorithms that uses node identifiers of the network as labels and propagates labels step by step through the neighbours until it reaches the end of community. To aid the propagation process, two node agents namely listener and speaker are developed to propagate and receive labels based on the designed rules to form communities.

6.3.   Multi-label Propagation Architecture

Label propagation process involves interaction among agents based on certain rules for proper propagation of labels. The propagation is carried out to solve a problem, in other words to attain a specific goal. Agents are defined with the roles to be played to carry out the process with the aim of detecting communities. Once agents are designed, various processes are formulated to detect communities from the network. The process involved in the designed system is pre-processing, propagation, updating and post-processing (Prabavathi and Thiagarasu 2014).

A node that listens to the labels of other adjacent nodes (i.e. neighbours of a node) in the network is treated as a listener. The set of neighbour nodes that propagates labels to the listening node is treated as speaker node. An agent that performs tasks such as treating a node as listener and invoking the communication process is called listening agent. The listening agent initiates the communication with the speaker node and invokes the propagation. An agent that resides in the speaker side, deciding the labels to be spread and start spreading the labels is called as speaker agent. In the proposed algorithm, during each iteration, a node is taken as a listener. The neighbours of listening node send one or more labels depending upon the probability of occurrence of that label. Hence, it differs from SLPA which sends only one label at each iteration. The listening node receives one or multiple labels from each speaker. But, in SLPA, a listener receives only one label from each speaker. Determining the order of the nodes for each iteration, is done randomly in the SLPA. In the proposed system, the order of nodes for propagation has been determined either through node identifiers or sorted nodes based on degree. There are two types of execution for label updating process: synchronous and asynchronous. In this research work, asynchronous updating has been used.

6.3.1.   Pre-processing and Initialization

Pre-processing

First the nodes of a network are loaded into a data structure. Every node in the network is initially assigned with only one label name. If the loaded network does not contain self-loops, then self-loop is added to change a node as neighbour to itself. Making a node as neighbour to itself helps to send its own label during propagation process trying to form communities under its name. Taking into account one's own label, makes the propagation process smooth as in SLPA and LabelRank algorithms (Xie et al. 2011b; Xie et al. 2013a). If the self loops are added the node degrees of each node in the network should be calculated.

Normally, labels are not passed from a node to all the nodes in the network. It is passed only to the neighbouring nodes based on specified rules. The nodes to which the labels should be passed at the starting of the iteration are determined by node degree. A node degree indicates the number of nodes adjacent to it. Storing the neighbour nodes in a memory for each node of the network is important. Without knowing the neighbour nodes, the algorithm cannot propagate labels in the network. Hence, to reduce the time complexity of calculating neighbours every time when it is placed in the propagation process, the neighbour list is calculated before the propagation process.

Initialization

The process of label propagation starts from any one of the node in the network. The node which requests for labels from its neighbouring nodes is called listener node. All the neighbours of a listening node act as speaker nodes. The first phase of propagation starts from deciding which node is going to act as listener? When one of the nodes among n nodes is selected as listener by the system, then all the neighbouring nodes start propagating labels to that listener. Updation of node labels takes place after the listener accepting the propagated labels. The important task is to decide which node is going to be the first listener among n nodes, the second listener and so on.

In social networks, if a user has maximum friend list in a group and if that user posts a message, it will be viewed by maximum friends. If one or all listeners start to propagate the posted message, then, that particular message spreads more in the network. The label of a node which has maximum node degree, spreads its labels faster than the label of a node which has less node degree. In reality, a person adopting a new idea tries to   follow a neighbour who has more connections to other neighbours because the neighbour who have more number of connections has higher number of potential sources of information (Xie and Szymaski 2011a). Based on the above idea, the order of propagation has been designed based on the node degrees. Various choices for determining the order of choosing the listener node are:

- Randomly select a node as a listener.
- Nodes are sorted in ascending order according to node labels (in case the labels are numbers). From the sorted list of labels, the order is determined.
- The nodes are sorted according to its degree from high to low. A node that has maximum degree acts as the first listener, then the next node and so on.

MLPA follows the second and third strategy. Every node stores the probabilities of labels what it observes as the propagation progresses. The nodes will not or cannot observe labels from all the nodes in the network. Initially, it listens to the labels sent by the neighbours only. The neighbour list of each node is designed either as a matrix representation or as a vector space. If the probabilities are initialized as matrix representation, space complexity is high, whereas vector space occupies less space. In this work, both designs were used for storing the probabilities. The following steps are performed for initializing label distribution memory:

- Select a node in the network.
- Calculate and assign initial probabilities for all the neighbours in the memory of the selected node (label distribution matrix or vector).
- Repeat steps 1 to 3 for all the nodes in the network.

If the label distribution is treated as matrix representation, then in step 2, for all the neighbours of a node, its initial probabilities are calculated and initialized. For the nodes that are not neighbours, the probabilities are initialized as zero. Initializing zeros makes the probability distribution to be sparse as propagation progresses. This can be avoided through vector representation as iteration progress or from the beginning of the process itself. If label distribution memory is represented as vectors, then each element of the vector contains label names and their corresponding probabilities.

6.3.2. Rules for Multi-label Propagation

Initially, if there are n number of nodes in the network, then, there are n number of communities. A multi-label propagation algorithm aims to propagate multiple labels between nodes in the network and maintains more than one label for a node indicating its strength of membership to multiple communities. The algorithm is comprised of three phases: 1. deciding which node is going to send the label 2.deciding which node is going to get the label and 3. how to update the label probabilities. The order of propagation is decided as designed in the initialization phase. Two agents, namely speaker and listener are designed for propagating labels. The received labels are not just updated immediately. An update condition is used in this system for deciding whether to accept the labels or retain the old labels. The functionalities of the communicating nodes are managed by following agents:

Speaker

The propagation starts with a speaker and listener node. A node acts both as speaker and listener depending on whether it is sending labels or receiving labels. In LPA, a node has only one label. Hence, it sends only that label name to its neighbour. In COPRA and SLPA, a node contains multiple labels as the intention of these algorithms is to detect overlapping communities. Even though a node has multiple labels in its memory, SLPA sends only one label to its neighbour using random selection. Due to this random selection, the algorithm is non-deterministic in nature. In order to overcome this limitation, two rules (Rule1 and Rule2) are designed for speaker agent. The main function of speaker agent is to decide which labels should be passed to the listening node, when listener agent waits for the labels from the speaker node. For deciding the labels speaker agent follows the rules:

Rule 1: If there are l labels stored in the probability distribution memory of node i and all labels have equal number of occurrence, i.e. no label has maximum frequency, then all the labels are sent to the listener.

Rule 2: If there are l labels stored in the memory of i and if p, q are labels that occur equally maximum than other labels, then both the labels p and q are sent to the listener.

Listener

The listener node is used to receive all the labels send by one or more speaker nodes and decide which labels to pass for updating process. The listener node holds as many labels as it likes depending on the underlying network structure and the knowledge accumulated repeatedly by observing the labels. It uses a memory to store all the received labels instead of erasing the previously stored labels. Each node has a memory and takes into account information that has been observed in the past to make current decisions. The more a node listens to a label, the more it spreads this label to other nodes. This nature is similar to that of people's behavior of spreading most frequently discussed opinions in social network. Hence, this type of label spreading algorithms is most suitable for complex networks, especially for social network.

A label propagation process always starts with a listener. The core task performed by the listener agent is the decision making process of which labels are to be accepted and which labels are to be omitted? If a node i contains j neighbours and if the number of labels send by j nodes to node i is stored in label list l, then, to determine what labels should be considered for updation, the following rules are designed:

Rule 1: If the label names in the list l are unique, i.e. all labels occurs only once, then, all the labels in the list l should be sent for updating process.

Rule 2: If labels in the list l are not unique, i.e. some labels occurs less number of times and the remaining labels occur more number of times, then, the following rules are applied:

(i) if one specific label has maximum number of occurrence (n) times among l labels and all other labels occur less than n times, then only one label that have maximum occurrence should be considered for updating process and all others should be ignored.

(ii)Assuming p and q are two label names in the label set l, and if both p and q occur maximum number of times and the number of occurrence of other labels except p and q are less than this count, both labels p and q are passed for updating process.

6.3.3. Label Updation and Termination

Algorithms such as COPRA and LPA do not consider the labels that have been observed in the past to take current decisions. SLPA accumulates knowledge of repeatedly observed labels instead of erasing all but one of them using memory for storing the labels. When a listener accepts multiple labels from the neighbouring nodes, the next critical question is how to maintain the accepted labels. The issues are:

- Whether the previously stored labels should be retained?
- Whether totally to forget the previous knowledge and store only the new labels?

In the proposed design, the approach followed by SLPA is adapted. When new labels are propagated to the listener, the listener maintains all the new labels with the previously stored labels. This is determined using a probabilistic approach. The probability of all selected labels is updated in the corresponding memory of the node only after performing a conditional check. For performing the condition check, similarities between the node labels are used after every propagation. If the conditional check is satisfied, the node is updated. Due to this updating process, the probabilities of labels change during each iteration. Depending upon these updating process, at a certain stage the communities are formed. In order to contract the propagation process, inflation operator used in LabelRank algorithm is used in this work. Inflation is used to detect the communities quickly. The contraction is performed by increasing the probabilities of labels which have maximum probabilities and decreasing the probabilities of labels which do not have maximum probability. When the inflation operator is applied to the probability distribution matrix or vector, the labels which have higher probabilities get more preference than the labels with lower probability.

In LPA, each node holds only a single label that is updated adopting the majority labels in the neighbourhood at the end of the iteration. At the end of the propagation process, disjoint communities are formed. The stop criterion used in LPA is every node is assigned to the most popular label in its neighbourhood. In COPRA, each node is allowed to possess multiple labels. SLPA also follows the same procedure by retaining multiple labels at the end of iteration. In SLPA, during each iteration, a speaker sends only one label and listener accepts only one label from the collection of labels received from multiple speakers. SLPA continues till it collects sufficient information for post processing or T iterations are reached.

In MLPA, the speaker and listener agents designed in this system accepts multiple labels from speaker and at the end of the propagation process; a node can hold multiple labels like COPRA and SLPA. The stop criterion of original LPA, does not suit for algorithms that follows multi-label propagation approach. A stop condition which is similar to that of LabelRank algorithm using a similarity measure is followed.

After an iteration is completed, a stop condition is checked. If the stop condition is true, then the iteration stops and to find the communities post-processing phase is to be performed. If the stop condition is false, the iteration continues until the specified number of times. If the predefined number of iteration is completed, then, post processing is performed or else, the propagation process continues until either the stop condition is satisfied or the maximum number of iterations specified is reached.

6.3.4. *Post-processing*

At the end of the iteration, only the label information that reflects the underlying network structure is present. The node labels are stored as probability representation of labels. The probability distribution denotes how strong a node belongs to a community. A threshold value is applied to the resultant probability of labels. The label of a node which is less than the threshold value is deleted from memory of that node. After the threshold procedure is over, the system groups the nodes having a particular label and forms a community. This is the only step performed in post-processing phase.

Normally, after applying threshold value, a node may contain one label. If so, the system is said to detect disjoint communities. If a node contains more than one label after applying threshold value, then the node belongs to more than one community. Such nodes are called overlapping nodes and the resultant communities are said to be overlapping. If the threshold value is too low, then the algorithm produces multiple communities. Conversely, if the threshold value is too high, communities may not be identified correctly. Post-processing refines the output in an acceptable manner.

In algorithms such as COPRA, a node belonging to number of maximal memberships is controlled by the parameters., but in MLPA the maximum number of membership of a node belonging to multiple communities is determined by the network structure and the rules designed. It does not depend on any parameter for restricting a node from belonging to multiple communities.

6.4.   Overall System Design

Input: Network $N = (V, E)$

Output: Community structure $C = \{C_1, C_2...C_P\}$

T: user defined maximum iteration

r: threshold for post processing

q: threshold for conditional update

in: inflation operator

1.   Give initial unique label names for each node (same as node id)
2.   Add self loop to all the nodes in the network
      Sort nodes in the order of the degree and store it in ordered vector
      Calculate initial probabilities such that equal probabilities are assigned for each neighbour and store it in label distribution matrix
3.   Repeat T times or until stop criterion satisfied
      All nodes in ordered vector are marked as unvisited
      repeat
      - Select a unvisited node
      - Each neighbour of the selected node sends a label or multiple labels based on the probability of occurrence (frequency) of labels in the memory based on speaking rule
      - Listener accepts one or more labels based on listening rule for updating process
      - If the update condition is satisfied, listener updates the probability of one or more labels and the listener is marked as visited. Inflation operator is applied to increase the probabilities of labels having maximum occurrence until all nodes in ordered vector are marked as visited
4.   Post-process the labels in the memory based on the threshold r and form the communities. If a node contains multiple labels, overlapping communities occur.

6.5.   Conclusion

Given a network, the aim of overlapping community detection algorithm is to find sub groups of nodes, such that a node exists in more than one community. In social network, a community is a group of people who are more similar to each other within the group than people outside the group. Assuming this basic idea that communities are essentially local structures, an algorithm that uses the network structure alone to guide its process and requires neither parameters nor objective functions to detect communities is designed. The single label propagation strategy used in SLPA has been modified to propagate multiple labels. COPRA uses multiple labels, but forces a belonging coefficient to limit the number of labels. This has been avoided in MLPA and it uses the features of SLPA and LabelRank algorithms. Agents are utilized to propagate and accept multiple labels and determine the labels for updating process which is controlled by the formulated rules. Two agents are designed with rules that restrict the unwanted labels for propagation and updation and it involves the coordination between speaker and listener agents for sharing the labels to form communities. The formulated rules help to avoid the non-deterministic communities and avoid the randomness in propagation process. The novelty of this approach is to consider not a single label for updating process but multiple labels based on update conditions.

The algorithm does not ask for any parameters regarding the number of communities to be detected beforehand. The listener and speaker agents detect the number of communities in the network using the process of label propagation alone. The inflation operator is used to contract the propagation and reduce the size of label distribution vector and the updating condition is used to detect termination based on scarcity of changes in the network. The threshold for post-processing is used to remove the labels with low probabilities. The inflation, updating condition and threshold parameters help the label propagation algorithm to detect communities quickly. Proper pre-processing helps to improve the detected quality of communities and initialization helps to reduce the time complexity of the algorithm. The conditional updating using similarity measures and inflation operators stabilizes the detected communities and avoid random outputs. Post-processing guides to group nodes with highest probabilities. The algorithm helps to identify overlapping nodes and overlapping communities in complex networks. In this book an overall view of complex networks and community detection has been given. The importance of the overlapping community detection research area has been discussed. A literature review of various disjoint and overlapping algorithms using label propagation technique has been reviewed and a modified label propagation approach is presented.

Glossary of Terms

Benchmark Networks	Graphs with known community structure
Betweenness centrality	A measure equal to the number of shortest paths from all vertices to all others that pass through that node.
Community	Densely interconnected subset of nodes inside networks A group of nodes within which the network connections are dense, but between which they are sparse
Community overlap	A node in a network belong to more than one community
Centrality	In network terminology, centrality of a node measures its relative importance within a graph.
CFinder	A program for obtaining k-clique communities
Cliques	Cliques are subgraphs in which every node is connected to every other node in the clique.
Clustering coefficient	In graph theory, it is a measure of the degree to which nodes in a graph tend to cluster together.
Complex network	A network with non-trivial topological features that do not occur in simple networks such as random graphs but often occur in real graphs.
Degree	The number of connections or edges the node has to other nodes.
Dendrogram	A tree diagram frequently used to illustrate the arrangement of the clusters produced by hierarchical clustering.
Disjoint communities	A community structure comprised of subgroup of nodes , where the node belongs to only one community
Labels	Unique node identifiers
Listener	A node in the network that gathers labels from neighbor nodes
Modularity (Q)	A benefit function that measures the quality of a particular division of a network into communities.
Monster community	A large community comprising the whole network

| **Null model** | It is a graph which matches one specific graph in some of its structural features, but which is otherwise taken to be an instance of a random graph. |

Null model
It is a graph which matches one specific graph in some of its structural features, but which is otherwise taken to be an instance of a random graph.

Normalized Mutual Information
A evaluation metrics that compares the detected communities with known partitions

Power law
A functional relationship between two quantities, where one quantity varies as a power of another.

Random graph
A graph that is generated by some random process where edges are distributed randomly

Real-world networks
Networks existing in the society

Scale free network
Class of networks whose degree distribution follows a power law

Speaker
A node that sends labels to the listener node

Small-world network
A network with most nodes are not neighbors of one another, but most nodes can be reached from every other by a small number of hops or steps.

Refers to an ensemble of networks in which the mean geodesic (i.e.,shortest-path) distance between nodes increases sufficiently slowly as a function of the number of nodes in the network.

Social Networks
A network of social interactions and personal relationships

Quality metrics
Function used to measure the quality of results (communities) obtained by the community detection algorithm.

INDEX

A

Adjacency matrix 27

Agents 40

Agglomerative 21

Asynchronous update 65

B

Benchmarks 42

C

Connectedness 38

Clique 7

Clique Percolation 31

Clustering coefficient 26

Complex Networks 1

Cutoff 60

D

Datasets 16

Deterministic 61

Degree distribution 2

Density function 36

Directed graphs 39

Disjoint Communities 9

Divisive 21

Dynamic Networks 17

E

Edges 1

Epidemic 3

External Optimization 23

F

Fitness Measure 8

Fuzzy 31

G

Global 66

Greedy optimization 23

H

Hierarchical communities 33

Hop attenuation 56

I

Inflation 29

Intrinsic communities 40

L

Labels 29

Latent communities 35

LFR Benchmarks 44

Listener 75

Local optimality 38

L-partition model 44

M

Modularity 8

Multipartite 19

Modules 5

N

Near linear time complexity 69

Node 76

Non-deterministic 63

Null model 8

O

Omega Index 49

Overlapping Communities 11

P

Parameter free 18

Path 4

Post processing 38

Potts Model 51

| Power law | 2 |
| Propagation | 30 |

S

Seed communities	36
Self loops	73
Similarity measures	9
Simulated Annealing	23
Small world network	1
Social Networks	1
Speaker	64
Spectral clustering	23
Static networks	18
Strong communities	7
Synthetic networks	28

T

| Time complexity | 3 |
| Threshold | 29 |

U

| Undirected | 31 |
| Unweighted | 32 |

V

| Variance | 35 |
| Vertices | 1 |

W

| Weak communities | 7 |
| Weighted | 9 |

REFERENCES

- Adamcsek B., Palla G., Farkas I.J., Derényi I., Vicsek T., CFinder: Locating cliques and overlapping modules in biological networks, Bioinformatics, Vol. 22, No. 8, Pp. 1021-1023, 2006.

- Ahn Y.Y., Bagrow J.P., Lehmann S., Link communities reveal multiscale complexity in networks, Nature, Vol. 466, No. 1, Pp. 761-764, 2010.

- Albert R., Barabasi A.L., Statistical Mechanics of complex networks, Review of Modern Physics, Vol. 74, No. 1, Pp. 47-97, 2002.

- Amaral L.A.N., Scala A., Barthelemy M., Stanley H.E., Classes of small world networks, Proceedings of the National Academy of Sciences of the United States of America, Vol. 97, No. 21, Pp. 11149-11152, 2000.

- Arenas A., Danon L., Díaz-Guilera A., Gleiser P.M., Guimerá R., Community analysis in social networks, The European Physics Journal B-Condensed matter and Complex Systems, Vol. 38, No. 2, Pp. 373-380, 2004.

- Arenas A., Diaz-Guilera A., Perez-Vicente C.J., Synchronization reveals topological scales in complex networks, Physical Review Letters, Vol. 96, No. 11, 2006.

- Arenas A., Fernandez A., Fortunato S., Gomez S., Motif-based communities in complex networks, Journal of Physics, Vol. 41, No. 22, 2008a.

- Arenas A., Fernandez A., Gomez S., Analysis of the structure of complex networks at different resolution levels, New Journal of Physics, Vol. 10, No. 5, 2008b.

- Asur S., Parthasarathy S., Ucar D., An Event-based Framework for characterizing the evolutionary behavior of interacting graphs, ACM Transactions on Knowledge Discovery from Data (TKDD), Vol. 3, No. 4, Pp. 1-16, 2009.

- Bagrow J.P., Bollt E.M., A local method for detecting communities, Physical Review E, Vol. 72, 2005.

- Barabási A.L., Albert R., Emergence of scaling in random networks, Science, Vol. 286, No. 5439, Pp. 509-512, 1999.

- Barabasi A.L., Albert R., Jeong H., Scale-free characteristics of random networks: The topology of the world-wide web, Physica A: Statistical Mechanics and its Applications, Vol. 281, No. 1-4, Pp. 69-77, 2000.

- Barnes J., Class and Committees in a Norwegian Island Parish, Human Relations, Vol. 7, Pp. 39-58, 1954.

- Baumes J., Goldberg M.K., Magdon-Ismail M., Wallace A., Discovering hidden groups in communication networks, IEEE International Conference on Intelligence and Security Informatics (ISI), Pp. 378-389, 2004.

- Baumes J., Goldberg M., Krishnamoorthy M., Magdon-Ismail M., Preston N., Finding communities by clustering a graph into overlapping subgraphs, Proceedings of IADIS Applied Computing, Pp. 97-104, 2005a.

- Baumes J., Goldberg M., Magdon-Ismail M., Efficient identification of overlapping communities, Lecture Notes in Computer Science (LNCS 3495), IEEE International Conference on Intelligence and Security Informatics (ISI), Pp. 27-36, 2005b.

- Bianconi G., Gulbahce N., Motter A.E., Local Structure of Directed Networks, Physical Review Letters, Vol. 100, 2008.

- Blondel V.D., Guillaume J.L., Lambiotte R., Lefebvre E., Fast unfolding of communities in large networks, Journal of Statistical Mechanics: Theory and Experiment, Vol. 10, Pp. 1-12, 2008.

- Boccaletti S., Latorab V., Morenod C.Y., Chavezf M., Hwanga D.U., Complex networks: Structure and dynamics, Physics Reports, Vol. 424, Pp. 175-308, 2006.

- Boettcher S., Percus A.G., Optimization with external dynamics, Physical Review Letters, Vol. 86, Pp. 5211-5214, 2001.

- Bradley S.R., Keith B.G., Detecting Overlapping Communities in Complex Networks Using Swarm Intelligence for Multi-threaded Label Propagation, Complex networks, Studies in Computational Intelligence, Vol. 424, Pp. 111-119, 2013.

- Brandes U., Delling D., Gaertler M., On modularity clustering, IEEE transactions on Knowledge and Data Engineering, Vol. 20, No. 2, Pp. 172-188, 2008.

- Breve F., Zhao L., Quiles M., Uncovering overlap community structure in complex networks using particle competition, Proceedings of International Conference on Artificial Intelligence, Pp. 619-628, 2009.

- Cai Y., Shi C., Dong Y., Ke Q., Wu B., A Novel Genetic Algorithm for Overlapping Community Detection, Proceedings of 7th International Conference on Advanced Data Mining and Applications, Vol. 7120, Pp. 97-108, 2011.

- Capocci A., Servedio V., Detecting communities in large networks, Physica A: Statistical Mechanics and its Applications, Vol. 352, No. 2-4, Pp. 669-676, 2005.

- Carrington P.J., Scott J., Wasserman S., Models and Methods in Social Network Analysis, Cambridge University Press, 2005.

- Cazabet R., Amblard F., Hanachi C., Detection of overlapping communities in dynamical social networks, Proceedings of IEEE International conference on Social Computing conference (SOCIALCOM), Pp. 309-314, 2010.
- Chen J., Hsu W., Lee M.L., Ng S.K., Increasing confidence of protein interactions using network topological metrics, Bioinformatics, Vol. 22, No. 16, Pp. 1998-2004, 2006.
- Chen W., Wang Y., Yang S., Efficient influence maximization in social networks, Proceedings of the 15th ACM SIGKDD International Conference on Knowledge Discovery and Data Mining, Pp. 199-208, 2009.
- Chen D., Shang M., Lv Z., Fu Y., Detecting overlapping communities of weighted networks via a local algorithm, Physica A, Vol. 389, No. 19, Pp. 4177-4187, 2010a.
- Chen W., Liu Z., Sun X., Wang Y., A game-theoretic framework to identify overlapping communities in social networks, Data Mining and Knowledge Discovery, Vol. 21, No. 2, Pp. 224-240, 2010b.
- Clauset A., Newman M.E.J., Moore C., Finding community structure in very large networks, Physical Review E, Vol. 70, No. 6, 2004.
- Clauset A., Finding local community structure in networks, Physical Review E, Vol. 72, No. 2, 2005.
- Clauset A., Moore C., Newman M.E.J., Statistical Network Analysis: Models, Issues, New Directions, Springer, Lecture Notes in Computer Science, Vol. 4503, Pp. 1-13, 2007.
- Clauset A., Moore C., Newman M.E.J., Hierarchical structure and the prediction of missing links in networks, Nature, Vol. 453, No. 7191, Pp. 98-101, 2008.
- Coscia M., Giannotti F., Pedreschi D., A classification for community discovery methods in complex networks, Statistical Analysis and Data Mining, Vol. 4, No. 5, Pp. 512-546, 2011.
- Coscia M., Rossetti G., Giannottiv F., Pedreschi D., DEMON: A local-first discovery method for overlapping communities, Proceedings of the 18th ACM SIGKDD International Conference on Knowledge Discovery and Data Mining, Pp. 615-623, 2012.
- Costa L., Percolations of complex networks, Physics Review E, Vol. 70, 2004.
- Danon L., Diaz-Guilera A., Duch J., Arenas A., Comparing community structure identification, Journal of Statistical Mechanics: Theory and Experiment, Vol. 9, 2005.
- Danon L., Diaz-Guilera A., Arenas A., The effect of size heterogeneity on community identification in complex networks, Journal of Statistical Mechanics: Theory and Experiment, Vol. 11, 2006.
- Derényi I., Palla G., Vicsek T., Clique Percolation in Random Networks, Physical Review Letters, Vol. 94, No. 16, Pp. 160-202, 2005.

- Donetti L., Munoz M.A., Detecting network communities: A new systematic and efficient algorithm, Journal of Statistical Mechanics:Theory and Experiment, Vol. 10, 2004.

- Dorogovtsev S.N., Mendes J.F., Samukhin A.N., Structure of growing networks with preferential linking, Physical Review Letters, Vol. 85, No. 21, Pp. 4633-4636, 2000.

- Dorogovtsev S.N., Mendes J.F.F., Evolution of networks, Advances in Physics, Vol. 51, Pp. 1079-1187, 2002.

- Duch J., Arenes A., Community detection in complex networks using external optimization, Physics Review E., Vol. 72, No. 2, 2005.

- Erdös P., Rényi A., On random graphs, Publications of Math., Debrecen, Pp. 290-297, 1959.

- Evans T., Lambiotte R., Line graphs, link partitions and overlapping communities, Physics Review E, Vol. 80, 2009.

- Evans T., Clique graphs and overlapping communities, Journal of Statistical Mechanics: Theory and Experiment, 2010.

- Farkas I., Abel D., Palla G., Vicsek T., Weighted network modules, New Journal of Physics, Vol. 9, No. 6, 2007.

- Flake G.W., Lawrence S., Giles C.L., Efficient identification of web communities, Proceedings of the 6th ACM SIGKDD International Conference on Knowledge Discovery and Data Mining, Pp. 150-160, 2000.

- Flake G.W., Lawrence S., Giles C.L., Coetzee F., Self-organization and identification of web communities, IEEE Computer, Vol. 35, No. 3, Pp. 66-71, 2002.

- Fortunato S., Barthelemy M., Resolution limit in community detection, Proceedings of the National Academy of Sciences of the United States of America, Vol. 104, No. 1, Pp. 36-41, 2007.

- Fortunato S., Castellano C., Community structure in graphs, 2007, Encyclopedia of Complexity and Systems Science, Springer, Pp. 1141-1163, 2009.

- Fortunato S., Community Detection in Graphs, Physics Reports, Vol. 486, No. 3-5, Pp. 75-174, 2010.

- Freeman L.C., A set of measures of centrality based on betweenness, Sociometry, Vol. 40, No. 1, Pp. 35-41, 1977.

- Garlaschelli D., Caldarelli G., Pietronero L., Universal scaling relations in food webs, Nature, Vol. 423, No. 6936, Pp. 165-168, 2003.

- Gibson D., Kleinberg J., Raghavan P., Inferring web communities from link topology, Proceedings of the 9th ACM conference on Hypertext and hypermedia, Pp. 225-234, 1998.

- Girvan M., Newman M.E.J., Community structure in social and biological networks, Proceedings of the National Academy of Sciences of the United States of America, Vol. 99, No. 12, Pp. 7821-7826, 2002.

- Goldberg M., Kelley S., Magdon-Ismail M., Mertsalov K., Wallace A., Finding overlapping communities in social networks, Proceedings of IEEE 2nd International conference on Social Computing (SOCIALCOM), Pp. 104-113, 2010.

- Granovetter M., The strength of weak ties, American Journal of Sociology, Vol. 78, No. 6, Pp. 1360-1380, 1973.

- Gregory S., An Algorithm to Find Overlapping Community Structure in Networks, Proceedings of the 11th European Conference on Principles and Practice of Knowledge Discovery in Databases (PKDD 2007), Lecture Notes in Computer Science (Lecture Notes in Artificial Intelligence), Vol. 4702, Springer-Verlag Publications, Pp. 91-102, 2007.

- Gregory S., A Fast Algorithm to Find Overlapping Communities in Networks, Proceedings of the European Conference on Machine Learning and Knowledge discovery in Databases, Lecture Notes in Computer Science, Vol. 5212, Pp. 408-423, 2008.

- Gregory S., Finding Overlapping Communities Using Disjoint Community Detection Algorithms, Complex Networks: CompleNet, Springer-Verlag Publications, Pp. 47-61, 2009.

- Gregory S., Finding overlapping communities in networks by label propagation, New Journal of Physics, Vol. 12, No. 10, 2010.

- Gregory S., Fuzzy overlapping communities in networks, Journal of Statistical Mechanics: Theory and Experiment, Vol. 2011, Pp. 1-18, 2011.

- Guimerà R., Sales-Pardo M., Amaral L.A.N., Modularity from fluctuations in random graphs and complex networks, Physical Review E, Vol. 70, No. 2, 2004.

- Guimera R., Amaral L.A.N., Functional cartography of complex metabolic networks, Nature, Vol. 433, No. 7028, Pp. 895-900, 2005.

- Guimerà R., Sales-Pardo M., Amaral L.A.N., Module identification in bipartite and directed networks, Physics Review E, Vol. 76, 2007.

- Gulbahce N., Lehmann S., The art of community detection, Bioessays, Vol. 30, Pp. 934-938, 2008.

- Hofman J.M., Wiggins C.H., Bayesian approach to network modularity, Physical Review Letters, Vol. 100, 2008.

- Hopcroft J., Khan O., Kulis B., Selman B., Tracking evolving communities in large linked networks, Proceedings of the National Academy of Sciences of the United States of America, Vol. 101, Pp. 5249-5253, 2004.

- Huang J., Sun H., Liu Y., Song Q., Weninger T., Towards Online Multi-resolution Community Detection in Large-Scale Networks, PLoS ONE, Vol. 6, No. 8, 2011.

- Jian Li., William K., Cheung., Jimming Liu., Li C.H., On discovering community trends in social networks, Proceedings of ACM International conference on Web Intelligence and Intelligent agent Technology (IEEE/WIC), Vol. 1, Pp. 230-237, 2009.

- Katsaros D., Pallis G., Stamos K., Vakali A., Sidiropoulos S., Manolopoulos Y., CDNs Content Outsourcing via Generalized Communities, IEEE Transactions on Knowledge and Data Engineering, Vol. 21, No. 1, Pp. 137-151, 2009.

- Kelley S., The existence and discovery of overlapping communities in large-scale networks, Ph.D. thesis, Rensselaer Polytechnic Institute, Troy, NY, 2009.

- Kelley S., Goldberg M., Magdon-Ismail., Mertsalov K., Wallace A., Defining and discovering communities in social networks, Handbook of optimization in complex networks, Pp. 139-168, 2012.

- Kernighan B.W., Lin S., An efficient heuristic procedure for partitioning graphs, Bell Systems Technical Journal, Vol. 49, No. 2, Pp. 291-308, 1970.

- Kim Y., Jeong H., Map equation for link communities, Physics Review E, Vol. 84, 2011.

- Kumpula J.M., Kivela M., Kaski K., Saramaki J., A Sequential algorithm for fast clique percolation, Physical Review E, Vol. 78, No. 2, 2008.

- Lancichinetti A., Fortunato S., Radicchi F., Benchmark graphs for testing community detection algorithm, Physical Review E, Vol. 78, No. 4, 2008.

- Lancichinetti A., Fortunato S., Benchmarks for testing community detection algorithms on directed and weighted graphs with overlapping communities, Physical Review E., Vol. 80, No. 1, 2009a.

- Lancichinetti A., Fortunato S., Community detection algorithms: A comparative analysis, Physical Review E, Vol. 80, No. 5, 2009b.

- Lancichinetti A., Fortunato S., Kertesz J., Detecting the overlapping and hierarchical community structure of complex networks, New Journal of Physics, Vol. 11, No. 3, 2009c.

- Lancichinetti A., Radicchi F., Ramasco J.J., Statistical significance of communities in networks, Physical Review E, Vol. 81, 2010.

- Lancichinetti A., Radicchi F., Ramasco J.J., Fortunato S., Finding statistically significant communities in networks, PLos One, Vol. 6, No. 4, 2011.

- Lazar A., Abel D., Vicsek T., Modularity measure of networks with overlapping communities, Europhysics Letters, Vol. 90, 2010.

- Leskovec J., Lang K.J., Mahoney M., Empirical comparison of algorithms for network community detection, Proceedings of the 19th International Conference on World Wide Web (WWW), Pp. 631–640, 2010.

- Leung I.X.Y., Hui P., Lip P., Crowcroft J., Towards real-time community detection in large networks, Physics Review E, Vol. 79, 2009.

- Lin Li., Shenghong Li., Hongjiao Li., Zhengmin X., Songnian L.A., Identification of Overlapping Communities by Label Propagation, Journal of Information and Computational Science, Vol. 9, No. 15, Pp. 4413-4419, 2012.

- Liu Y., Luo J., Yang H., Liu L., Finding closely communicating community based on ant colony clustering model, Proceedings of the International Conference on Artificial Intelligence and Computational Intelligence, Vol. 3, Pp. 127-131, 2010.

- Liu D., Jin D., He D., Yang J., Yang B., Community mining in complex networks, Journal of Computer Research and Development, Vol. 50, No. 10, Pp. 2140-2154, 2013.

- Lusseau D., Schneider K., Boisseau O.J., Haase P., Slooten E., Dawson S.M., The bottlenose dolphin community of doubtful sound features a large proportion of long-lasting associations, Behavioral Ecology and Sociobiology, Vol. 54, No. 4, Pp. 396-405, 2003.

- Lusseau D., Newman M.E.J., Identifying the role that individual animals play in their social network, Proceedings of the Royal Society of London Series B: Biological Sciences, Vol. 271, Pp. 477-481, 2004.

- Lynch N. A., Distributed Algorithms, Morgan Kaufmann Publishers, 1996.

- Milo R., Shen-Orr S., Itzkovitz S., Kashtan N., Chklovskii D., Alon U., Network motifs: simple building blocks of complex networks, Science, Vol. 298, No. 5594, Pp. 824-827, 2002.

- Moody J., White D., Structural cohesion and embeddedness: A hierarchical concept of social groups, American Journal of Sociology, Vol. 107, No. 3, Pp. 679-716, 2003.

- Moore C., Newman M.E.J., Epidemics and percolation in small-world networks, Physical Review E, Vol. 61, No. 5, 2000.

- Mucha P.J., Richardson T., Macon K., Porter M.A., Onnela J., Community Structure in time-dependent, multiscale, multiplex networks, Science, Vol. 328, Pp. 876-878, 2010.

- Nepusz T., Petrocz A., Negyessy L., Bazso F., Fuzzy communities and the concept of bridgeness in complex networks, Physical Review E, Vol. 77, 2008.

- Newman M.E.J., The Structure of Scientific Collaboration Networks, Proceedings of the National Academy of Sciences of the United States of America, Vol. 98, No. 2, Pp. 404-409, 2001.

- Newman M.E.J., The Structure and function of complex networks, Society of Industrial and Applied Mathematics (SIAM) Review, Vol. 45, No. 2, Pp. 167-256, 2003.
- Newman M.E.J., Fast algorithm for detecting community structure in networks, Physical Review E, Vol. 69, No. 6, 2004.
- Newman M.E.J., Girvan M., Finding and Evaluating Community Structure in Networks, Physical Review E, Vol. 69, No. 2, 2004.
- Newman M.E.J., Barabási A.L., Watts D.J., The structure and dynamics of networks, Princeton University Press, 2006a.
- Newman M.E.J., Finding community structure in networks using the eigenvectors of matrices, Physical Review E, Vol. 74, No. 3, 2006b.
- Newman, M.E.J., Modularity and Community Structure in Networks, In Proceedings of the National Academy of Sciences of United States of America, Vol. 103, No. 23, Pp. 8577-8582, 2006c.
- Nguyen N.P., Dinh T.N., Dung T., Thai M.T., Overlapping community structures and their detection on social networks, Proceedings of IEEE International conference on Social Computing (SOCIALCOM), 2011.
- Nicosia V., Mangioni G., Carchiolo V., Malgeri M., Extending the definition of modularity to directed graphs with overlapping communities, Journal of Statistical Mechanics: Theory and Experiment, Vol. 3, 2009.
- Onnela J.P., Saramäki J., Kert'esz J., Kaski K., Intensity and coherence of motifs in weighted complex networks, Physical Review E, Vol. 71, 2005.
- Padrol-Sureda A., Perarnau-Llobet G., Pfeifle J., Munts-Mulero V., Overlapping community search for social networks, Proceedings of International Conference on Data Engineering, Pp. 992-995, 2010.
- Palla G., Derenyi I., Farkas I., Vicsek T., Uncovering the overlapping community structure of complex networks in nature and society, Nature, Vol. 435, No. 7043, Pp. 814-818, 2005.
- Palla G., Farkas J., Pollner P., Derenyi I., Vicsek T., Directed Network modules, New Journal of Physics, Vol. 9, No. 6, Pp. 186-207, 2007a.
- Palla G., Barabási A.L., Vicsek T., Quantifying social group evolution, Nature, Vol. 446, nO. 713, Pp. 664-667, 2007b.
- Pastor-Satorras R., Vespignani A., Epidemic spreading in scale-free networks, Physical Review Letters, Vol. 86, No. 14, Pp. 3200-3203, 2001.
- Pollner P., Palla G., Vicsek T., Preferential Attachment of Communities: The Same Principle, but a Higher Level, Europhysics Letters, Vol. 73, No. 3, Pp. 478-484, 2006.

- Pons P., Latapy M., Computing communities in large networks using random walks, Journal of Graph Algorithms and Applications, Vol. 10, No. 2, Pp. 191-218, 2006.
- Pons P., Latapy M., Post-processing hierarchical community structures: quality improvements and multi-scale view, Theoretical Computer Science, Vol. 412, No. 8-10, Pp. 892-900, 2011.
- Porter M.A., Onnela J.P., Mucha P.J., Communities in networks, Notices of the American Mathematical Society, Vol. 56, No. 9, Pp. 1082-1097, 2009.
- Prabavathi G.T., Thiagarasu V., Meenakshi S., Modeling Autonomy Based Overlapped Community Detection Algorithm in Complex Networks, Proceedings of Centenary Session of Indian Science Congress (ICT), Pp. 63-64, 2013a, .
- Prabavathi G.T., Thiagarasu V., A Review on Overlapping Community Detection Algorithms, International Journal of Applied Research and Studies, Vol. 2, No. 3, Pp. 347-352, 2013b.
- Prabavathi G.T., Thiagarasu V., Overlapping Community Detection Algorithms in Dynamic Networks: An Overview, International Journal of Emerging Technologies in Computational and Applied Sciences, Vol. 6, No. 4, Pp. 299-303, 2013c.
- Prabavathi G.T., Thiagarasu V., Design and Development of Overlapping Community Detection Algorithm using Multi-Label Propagation, International Journal of Advance Research in Computer Science and Management Studies, Vol. 2, No. 2, Pp. 195-199, 2014.
- Psorakis I., Roberts S., Ebden M., Sheldon B., Overlapping community detection using Bayesian non-negative matrix factorization, Physical Review E, Vol. 83, 2011.
- Radicchi F., Castellano C., Cecconi F., Loreto V., Parisi D., Defining and identifying communities in networks, Proceedings of the National Academy of Sciences of the United States of America, Vol. 101, No. 9, Pp. 2658-2663, 2004.
- Radicchi F., Lancichinetti A., Ramasco J., Combinatorial approach to modularity, Physical Review E, Vol. 82, 2010.
- Raghavan U.N., Albert R., Kumara S., Near linear time algorithm to detect community structures in large-scale networks, Physical Review E, Vol. 76, No. 3, 2007.
- Ravasz E., Somera A.L., Mongru D.A., Oltvai N., Hierarchical organization of modularity in metabolic networks, Science, Vol. 297, No. 5586, Pp. 1551-1555, 2002.
- Rees B.S., Gallagher, Overlapping community detection by collective friendship group inference, Proceedings of International Conference on Advances in Social Network Analysis and Mining, Pp. 375-379, 2010.
- Reichardt J., Bornholdt S., Detecting fuzzy community structures in complex networks with a potts model, Physical Review Letters, Vol. 93, No. 21, 2004.

- Reichardt J., Bornholdt S., Statistical mechanics of community detection, Physics Review E, Vol. 74, No. 1), 2006.
- Rosvall M., Bergstrom C.T., An information-theoretic framework for resolving community structure in complex networks, Proceedings of the National Academy of Sciences of the United States of America, Vol. 104, No. 18, Pp. 7327-7331, 2007.
- Rosvall M.B., Maps of random walks on complex networks reveal community structure, Proceedings of the National Academy of Sciences of the United States of America, Vol. 105, No. 4, Pp. 1118-1123, 2008.
- Sales-Pardo M., Guimer`a R., Moreira A.A., Amaral L.A.N., Extracting the hierarchical organization of complex systems, Proceedings of the National Academy of Sciences of the United States of America, Vol. 104, No. 39, Pp. 15224-15229, 2007.
- Schaeffer S.E., Graph clustering, Computer Science Review, Vol. 1, 2007, pp. 27-64.
- Scott J.P., Social Network Analysis: A Handbook, SAGE Publications, 2000.
- Shen H., Cheng X., Cai K., Hu M-B., Detect overlapping and hierarchical community structure in networks, Physica A: Statistical Mechanics and its Applications, Vol. 388, No. 8, Pp. 1706 -1712, 2009a, .
- Shen H., Cheng X., Guo J., Quantifying and identifying the overlapping community structure in networks, Journal of Statistical Mechanics: Theory and Experiment, Vol. 7, 2009b.
- Strogatz S.H., Exploring complex networks, Nature, Vol. 410, Pp. 268-276, 2001.
- Subelj L., Bajec M., Unfolding communities in large complex networks:Combining defensive and offensive label propagation for core extraction, Physical Review E, Vol. 83, No. 3, 2011.
- Tibely G., Kertesz J., On the equivalence of the label propagation method of community detection and a potts model approach, Physica A, Vol. 387, Pp. 4982-4984, 2008.
- Tyler J.R., Wilkinson D.M., Huberman B.A., Email as spectroscopy: Automated discovery of community structure within organizations, Proceedings of the 1st International Conference on Communities and Technologies, Pp. 81-96, 2003.
- Van Dongen S., Graph Clustering by Flow Simulation, Ph.D. thesis, Dutch National Research Institute for Mathematics and Computer Science, University of Utrecht, Netherlands, 2000.
- Wang X., Chen G., Lu H., A very fast algorithm for detecting community structures in complex networks, Physica A: Statistical Mechanics and its Applications, Vol. 384, No. 2, Pp. 667-674, 2007.
- Wang X., Jiao L., Wu J., Adjusting from disjoint to overlapping community detection of complex networks, Physica A, Vol. 388, Pp. 5045-5056, 2009.

- Wang Q., Fleury E., Fuzzy community structure and modular overlaps, Studies in Mining Social Networks and Security Informatics (SNSI), Springer Verlag Publications, 2012.

- Watts D.J., Strogatz S.H., Collective dynamics of small-world networks, Nature, Vol. 393, Pp. 440-442, 1998.

- Watts D.J., Dodds P.S., Newman M.E.J., Identity and search in social networks, Science, Vol. 296, Pp. 1302-1305, 2002.

- Wasserman S., Faust K., Social Network Analysis: Methods and Applications, Structural Analysis in the Social Sciences, Cambridge University Press, Cambridge, 1994.

- Wei F., Qian W., Wang C., Zhou A., Detecting overlapping community structures in networks, World Wide Web, Vol. 12, No. 2, Pp. 235-261, 2009.

- Wei Hu., Finding statistically significant communities in networks with weighted label propagation, Social Networking, Vol. 2, Pp. 138-146, 2013.

- White S., Smyth P., A spectral clustering approach to finding communities in graphs, Proceedings of the SIAM International Conference on Data Mining, Society of Industrial and Applied Mathematics Pp. 274-285, 2005.

- Wilkinson D., Huberman B.A., A method for finding communities of related genes, Proceedings of Natural Academy of Sciences of the United States of America, Vol. 101, Pp. 5241-5248, 2004.

- Wu F. Y., The Potts model, Review of Modern Physics, Vol. 54, No. 1, Pp. 235-268, 1982.

- Wu F., Huberman B., Finding communities in linear time: a Physics approach, The European Physics Journal B, Vol. 38, No. 2, Pp. 331-338, 2004.

- Wu Z., Lin Y., Gregory S., Balanced multi-label propagation for overlapping community detection in social networks, Journal of Computer Science and Technology, Vol. 27, No. 3, Pp. 468-479, 2012

- Xie J., Szymanski B.K, Community detection using a neighborhood strength driven label propagation algorithm, Proceedings of IEEE Network Science Workshop, Pp. 188-195, 2011a.

- Xie J., Szymanski B.K., Liu X., SLPA: Uncovering Overlapping Communities in Social Networks via a Speaker-listener Interaction Dynamic Process, Proceedings of IEEE ICDM Workshop on Data Mining Technologies for Computational Collective Intelligence (DMCCI), Pp. 344-349, 2011b.

- Xie J., Szymanski B.K., Towards linear time overlapping community detection in social networks, Proceedings of Advances in Knowledge Discovery and Data Mining (PAKDD), Pp. 25-36, 2012.

- Xie J., Szymanski B.K., LabelRank: A stabilized Label Propagation Algorithm for Community Detection in Networks, Proceedings of IEEE Network Science Workshop, Pp. 138-143, 2013a.
- Xie J., Kelley S., Szymanski B., Overlapping Community Detection in Networks: The State of the Art and Comparative Study, ACM Computing Surveys, Vol. 45, No. 4, Pp. 1-35, 2013b.
- Zachary W., An Information Flow Model for Conflict and Fission in Small Groups, Journal of Anthropological Research, Vol. 33, No. 4, Pp. 452-473, 1977.
- Zhang S., Wang R.S., Zhang X.S., Identification of overlapping community structure in complex networks using fuzzy c-means clustering, Physica A, Vol. 374, Pp. 483-490, 2007.
- Zhang X.S., Wang R. S., Wang Y., Wang J., Qiu Y., Wang L., Chen L., Modularity optimization in community detection of complex networks, European Physics Letters, Vol. 87, No. 3, 2009.